Prince Interpreted for E-Commerce

How Digital Merchants Gain Influence and Dominate Platforms

ANCIENT WISDOM HACKS

Third Edition

Table of Contents

Introduction: Why Machiavelli Matters in Ecommerce

Machiavelli wrote *The Prince* not as a moral guide, but as a manual for survival and dominance. At its core, the book strips power down to its brutal mechanics: how to gain it, how to keep it, and how to wield it effectively when the stakes are high. Machiavelli didn't care for ideals or theory — he cared for outcomes. He wrote, "A man who wishes to make a vocation of being good at all times will come to ruin among so many who are not good." In other words: nice guys finish last, especially when the world doesn't play fair.

His core ideas revolve around **power**, **pragmatism**, **control**, and **perception**. Power, to Machiavelli, isn't granted — it's seized. Those who wait for ideal conditions lose to those who move fast and adapt. Pragmatism means making the hard call when it benefits the greater goal. It's the willingness to do what works, even if it's unpopular. Control is about structure — building systems and taking responsibility for every detail. And perception? It's everything. "Everyone sees what you appear to be, few experience what you really are." Appear strong, stable, and confident, even when things behind the curtain are chaotic.

Now look at the Amazon marketplace. It's a modern battlefield — not of swords and fortresses, but of margins, listings, ads, and reviews. It's saturated. Thousands of sellers enter each day. It's ruthless. A single negative review or a hijacked Buy Box can ruin a product launch. And it's fast-changing. What works today might get your account suspended tomorrow.

In this world, idealism loses. Sellers who think quality alone will win, or who ignore branding and perception, get buried under the avalanche of better-prepared competitors. Machiavelli understood this. He didn't preach morality. He preached survival. He understood that leaders must make hard choices to protect what they've built. That principle applies directly to today's entrepreneurs.

This book delivers **realpolitik for Amazon sellers**. No fluff. No motivational clichés. Just strategy. Every chapter is focused on action — how to outsmart, outmaneuver, and outlast. How to build an Amazon business that not only survives but dominates, regardless of how the terrain shifts. The rules of ecommerce may be modern, but the game is as old as power itself. Machiavelli laid out the playbook. Now it's time to use it.

Chapter 1: Claiming Territory (Launching Your Amazon Brand)

"It is much safer to be feared than loved, if one must choose."
— Niccolò Machiavelli, *The Prince*

Launching your Amazon brand isn't just about selling a product. It's about claiming ground in a brutal and fast-moving battlefield. On Amazon, your competition isn't sitting idle. New sellers are entering every day. Algorithms are shifting without warning. Buyers are impatient and brutal. And success doesn't go to the most virtuous seller — it goes to the one who moves first, strikes hard, and builds fast.

When Machiavelli said it is safer to be feared than loved, he wasn't advocating cruelty for cruelty's sake. He was explaining a simple principle of power: strength earns survival. When you're launching your brand, you have two options — quietly try to enter a space and hope for love, or launch with intent, force, and domination, commanding attention and pushing others out of your way. The second path, while harder, is the one that wins in the long run. On Amazon, obscurity is death. Attention is oxygen. Aggression wins.

Let's break that down.

STAND OUT OR DIE INVISIBLE

The average Amazon buyer doesn't care how hard you worked on your product. They don't care about your story. They care about value, trust, and speed. If you can't win their attention in three seconds of scrolling, they move on. And that's where Machiavelli's principle kicks in. If you're launching quietly, hoping to build a slow organic following without ruffling feathers, you will lose. You'll be invisible. Instead, you need to *own* your niche from day one.

To "be feared" on Amazon means becoming the brand that competitors don't want to go up against. That fear can come from many places — better branding, sharper pricing, massive ad spend, or an overwhelmingly optimized listing. Fear is about appearing more capable, more prepared, and more dominant than those around you. Even if you're not the biggest seller yet, if you *look* like you're ready to take the whole category, many will retreat rather than risk a fight.

This doesn't mean being unethical. It means being bold, fast, and clear in your strategy.

NICHE SELECTION AS CONQUEST

In *The Prince*, Machiavelli wrote at length about newly acquired territories — how fragile they are, how much resistance they provoke, and what a ruler must do to hold them. Think of your product's niche the same way. When you enter a category, you are invading someone else's established space. Your goal is not just to survive there. Your goal is to take control.

Most sellers make the mistake of choosing niches based on surface-level data: high search volume, strong sales, low competition. But they fail to dig deeper. What they should be asking is: **Where are the weaknesses?** Where are the incumbent sellers getting lazy? Which products have terrible imagery? Who is ranking high but sitting on bad reviews? What listings are full of keyword gaps, poor bullet points, or weak branding?

These weaknesses are your entry points.

Machiavelli advised new rulers to identify weaknesses in existing regimes and exploit them to consolidate power. Apply that to Amazon: don't go for the biggest category. Go for the weakest stronghold. The one where your brand can come in with sharper images, better design, stronger messaging, and take ground before anyone notices what's happening.

And don't try to be everything at once. Machiavelli wrote, "A wise prince must devise means by which his citizens will always and in every sort of circumstance have need of his government." That means: specialize. Make your brand *necessary* to the niche you're entering. Don't be a general kitchen brand. Be *the* brand for minimalist, space-saving cooking tools for small apartments. Don't sell "travel accessories." Be the brand that owns the carry-on comfort category.

You're not building a product. You're building a kingdom. And every kingdom needs a strong claim to its land.

MOVE FAST OR GET SURROUNDED

Speed is everything.

When Machiavelli discussed the acquisition of new states, he emphasized the importance of *acting quickly before opposition can organize*. In Amazon terms, that means launching before the market catches on. If you've identified a gap in the category, don't sit on it. Waiting to perfect every detail will almost always mean someone else gets there first.

Sellers who wait for "ideal conditions" lose to sellers who take fast, decisive action.

This is where the landgrab mentality comes in. When you see opportunity, act. Order samples. Build your listing before inventory arrives. Launch with ads on day one. Activate Vine. Drive external traffic. Push for reviews. Lock down rank. Once you're in, you fortify — just like Machiavelli advised newly installed rulers to "occupy" territory swiftly and then build walls, alliances, and defenses to hold it.

In the early days of a product launch, you're most vulnerable. You're at zero reviews. Your listing hasn't earned Amazon's trust. The algorithm is watching you closely. This is your window to overwhelm the system — not cautiously step forward. You need momentum. You need orders flowing. You need to make it *look* like your product is the obvious choice, even before the market confirms it.

Fear, in this context, is created by momentum. A competitor scrolling through their tools and seeing a brand-new ASIN rising rapidly in rank, stacked with great imagery and a compelling price point, feels pressure. They might pause their own launch. They might raise their bid ceiling. They might exit the category altogether. If you move fast enough, you can shake the confidence of the other rulers on the map.

Remember: the longer you wait, the more the category evolves without you. Competitors patch their weak listings. Review counts rise. Costs increase. The opportunity window shrinks. Machiavelli didn't just preach action — he demanded it: "The opportunity that makes a man great is often a short one."

BUILDING A BRAND THAT SIGNALS DOMINANCE

Every inch of your listing signals something to your competitors and customers. If you look half-built, hesitant, or lazy, no one will take you seriously. But if your listing is sharp — perfect images, clear benefits, focused language — you send a different signal: *this seller is here to take over.*

Branding is your flag. Raise it high. Don't hide behind generic names, weak logos, or bland packaging. A strong brand tells the market you're not a hobbyist. You're building something long-term. And that alone can trigger a psychological shift — competitors become more cautious, customers become more loyal, and you gain the benefit of the doubt in an environment that rarely gives second chances.

This isn't about spending more. It's about strategic clarity. Machiavelli said, "It is better to act and repent than not to act and regret." Make bold choices. Use a color scheme that stands out. Lead with your strongest differentiator. Frame your first image like an ad, not a catalog photo. Show that you know exactly who you're speaking to, and why you're different from everyone else in the category.

When you claim territory, claim it loudly.

TACTICS FOR A DOMINANT LAUNCH

Let's put strategy into practice.

1. **Pick your battle wisely.**
   Don't chase high-volume markets blindly. Find segments where the top competitors are vulnerable. Use tools like Helium10 or Jungle Scout not just to look at revenue but to spot signs of decay — slow review velocity, generic branding, flat imagery.

2. **Strike early, strike hard.**
   Launch with everything ready. Keywords optimized. Imagery tested. Ads lined up. If you're not ready to go all-in on day one, you're not ready to launch.

3. **Manufacture fear.**
   Dominate visually. Outperform on listings. Get early reviews fast. Create the sense that you're bigger, better, and more advanced than you actually are. That

intimidation factor slows down competitors and buys you
time to fortify.

4. **Lock in the win.**
   Once you have momentum, don't coast. Scale your ad
   budget. Expand variations. Leverage bundles. Create
   defensible positions — trademark your brand, get Brand
   Registry, protect your listing from hijackers. Build moats.

5. **Control the narrative.**
   Push your brand story. Show up outside of Amazon. Use
   influencers, TikTok, blogs. Don't let your identity be defined
   only by a product photo. Make your customers part of a
   bigger story — one you control.

Machiavelli understood that survival wasn't about having the moral
high ground. It was about understanding the game better than
anyone else. He wrote *The Prince* not for the safe or the
soft-hearted — but for those who wanted to win.

FINAL THOUGHTS: THIS IS WAR

Launching on Amazon today is not like opening a lemonade stand.
It's war. It's politics. It's about power, attention, speed, and
survival. There is no prize for second place in a crowded category.
There is no trophy for being liked if you're not making money. And
there are no guarantees.

But there are patterns. And the patterns favor those who move with purpose, who strike with strength, and who build with clarity.

In the eyes of Machiavelli, fortune favors the bold, the prepared, and the ruthless. If you want to succeed on Amazon, don't wait for approval. Don't wait to be invited. Don't wait until you feel "ready."

Claim territory. Claim it now. Claim it like you mean to keep it.

Chapter 2: The New Prince (First-Time Sellers in the Arena)

"He who becomes prince through the favor of the people must always keep them friendly."
— Niccolò Machiavelli, *The Prince*

Stepping into the Amazon marketplace as a first-time seller is like seizing a throne in a land that doesn't know your name. You may have ambition, a good product, and even a few allies, but make no mistake: you're still a *new prince*—untested, vulnerable, and closely watched. Your first moves will define your rule. If they're weak or hesitant, your business may never gain traction. But if they're calculated and strategic, you can establish control quickly and build a brand that commands respect.

Machiavelli understood this dilemma intimately. In *The Prince*, he devoted much of his writing to the challenges new rulers face. They are rarely trusted. Their claim to power is often viewed with suspicion. Their grip is tenuous. Their enemies, both visible and hidden, wait for missteps. In Amazon terms, this means your brand isn't trusted by customers, doesn't yet have the algorithm on its side, and is entering a space full of sellers who would be happy to see you fail.

This chapter is about how to behave like a wise new prince in a hostile arena — how to build legitimacy, control perception, and avoid the critical early mistakes that destroy empires before they're born.

NEW BRANDS, OLD SKEPTICISM

Let's start with a brutal truth: customers do not trust you.

You're new. You have no reviews. You have no name. Your logo might look nice, but no one knows what it stands for. Every customer scrolling through your listing is trying to answer a single question: *"Can I trust this brand?"*

Machiavelli warned that a new ruler's first priority is to secure the loyalty of the people — not with promises, but with results. "It is necessary for a prince, if he wants to maintain his position, to learn how not to be good." In other words, you don't earn trust with good intentions. You earn it by being effective.

Effectiveness on Amazon starts with **reviews, branding, and social proof**. These are your tools to manufacture credibility where none exists. You don't have years of reputation to rely on. But you do have tactics. And Machiavelli would remind you that tactics — when used intelligently — can achieve in weeks what others take years to earn.

REVIEWS: THE MODERN CURRENCY OF TRUST

In Machiavelli's time, power was measured by territory, soldiers, and alliances. On Amazon, power is measured by the number and quality of your reviews. A listing with 2,000 positive reviews looks untouchable. One with zero looks like a gamble.

To a customer, reviews act like public endorsements. And early on, your job is to get them by any ethical means necessary.

Launch programs like Amazon Vine can help you seed those first reviews fast. If you're brand registered and your product is enrolled, Vine allows a select group of trusted reviewers to try your product in exchange for honest feedback. These reviews are brutally honest, which can hurt — but they also build legitimacy.

Outside Amazon, you can also encourage reviews through packaging inserts (within Amazon's Terms of Service), email follow-ups, and a stellar customer experience. But the point is this: you can't wait for reviews to happen organically. You need them early, and you need them consistently.

Machiavelli wrote, "A wise prince must rely on what he controls, not on the goodwill of others." Apply that to reviews. Don't rely on chance. Build a system that encourages reviews as part of every transaction.

BRANDING: YOUR ROYAL SEAL

Next comes branding. Think of this as your royal insignia — your flag, your colors, your identity. A strong brand communicates that you're not just here to sell a single product. You're building something long-term. And that stability is attractive to customers who don't want to waste time or money on a gamble.

A logo is not a brand. Nor is a clever name. Branding is a complete system of perception. It's the tone of your copy, the consistency of your visuals, the emotional feeling your storefront evokes. It's the difference between a random Amazon product and one that looks like it came from a trusted company, even if that company didn't exist three months ago.

The new prince must *look* like he belongs on the throne, even before everyone accepts him. On Amazon, that means your branding must project professionalism from day one. Invest in clean packaging, a consistent visual identity, a smart product title structure, and images that tell a story.

You want your brand to be the one customers feel confident recommending to a friend. That doesn't happen by accident. It happens when every touchpoint — from product photography to bullet points — tells the same coherent story. One of reliability, value, and purpose.

SOCIAL PROOF: BUILDING A FOLLOWING BEFORE YOU NEED IT

Social proof is the psychological phenomenon where people look to others to decide what's good. If everyone else is buying something, it must be worth buying. If a product has thousands of likes, comments, or reviews, it must be working.

A new prince needs to look like he has the support of the people. Even if the crowd isn't real yet, the illusion of momentum can often bring real momentum. This is why early outreach — to influencers, niche communities, and micro-audiences — is so powerful. When others are seen using and talking about your product, you instantly become more credible.

Use platforms like Instagram, TikTok, and Reddit not to hard sell, but to build buzz. Showcase your product being used. Tell stories. Highlight your mission. Tag customers. Feature real feedback. A brand that shows up outside Amazon looks more legit *inside* Amazon.

Machiavelli put it plainly: "The best fortress which a prince can possess is the affection of his people." In ecommerce, affection comes from visibility, relatability, and social momentum.

CONTROL PERCEPTION EARLY

The first impression you make will shape every customer's decision. This is why controlling your narrative from day one is essential.

Let's be clear: no one is going to read your entire listing. They're going to skim your images, glance at your reviews, check your star rating, and maybe glance at the bullet points. That's your window. That's your chance to shape how they see you.

That means your imagery must carry 80% of the weight. Your main image needs to stop the scroll. Your second and third images should show your product in context. The next should highlight differentiators — not just features, but *benefits*. What pain does your product solve? What convenience does it deliver? What makes it unique?

Your A+ Content (if you're brand registered) is where your brand story can come alive. Use this space to reinforce your mission, your quality promise, and your customer-first focus. Don't fill it with generic jargon. Tell a tight, focused story. You're not Apple yet, but act like a brand that knows where it's going.

A good brand story does one thing above all: it creates **confidence**.

Customers don't want to gamble. They want to feel reassured. Show them that you've thought this through. Show them that your product has been built with care. Show them that others like them have used it and been satisfied.

AVOIDING EARLY MISTAKES THAT COST TRUST

Machiavelli warned of the dangers of poor early decisions. "A prince who does not lay his foundations beforehand may with great ability lay them afterwards, but they will be laid with trouble to the architect and danger to the building." In other words: if you screw up your early moves, fixing them later will be expensive and painful.

For first-time sellers, here are the landmines that can derail your entire brand before it even starts:

1. **Poor Listing Quality**
    A sloppy listing signals a careless seller. Typos, vague bullets, bad photos, and keyword stuffing damage credibility fast. Remember: customers *assume* the product is as good as the listing. If the listing looks lazy, they assume the product is too.

2. **Underpricing Too Fast**
    It's tempting to undercut the competition to gain traction. And while short-term price drops can help build velocity, long-term price suppression is hard to recover from. If you enter too low, you signal that your product isn't worth much — and raising your price later becomes difficult.

3. **Ignoring Customer Messages and Reviews**
    New sellers often underestimate how closely the algorithm watches early buyer behavior. If you ignore negative reviews or fail to respond to customer concerns, your account metrics will suffer — and so will your ability to rank and convert.

4. **Weak Inventory Planning**
    Running out of stock early can destroy your ranking momentum. It tells Amazon you're unreliable. A prince cannot abandon his post. Make sure you have enough inventory to ride out your launch window and the first wave of traction.

5. **Launching Without a Strategy**
    Don't wing it. Every move should be part of a broader plan — keyword strategy, pricing tiers, ad campaigns, influencer outreach, review targets. A prince who reacts to every

problem without a plan quickly finds himself overthrown.

THE MINDSET OF A NEW PRINCE

You only get to launch once. And how you launch defines how the marketplace sees you.

Machiavelli wrote that "the wise man does at once what the fool does finally." Translation: be prepared. Move with intent. Don't just launch a product — install a brand. Build a system that generates trust, nurtures loyalty, and projects confidence from day one.

This means thinking like a ruler even when you're just getting started. Your early customers are your citizens. Your listing is your palace. Your images are your public address. Your packaging is your royal decree. Treat each with care. Control the optics. Control the story.

Yes, you're vulnerable. But vulnerability is only dangerous if you act like you have something to hide. If you carry yourself like a brand that deserves the crown, others will start to believe it. And once you've earned that belief, everything becomes easier — ad performance, review rate, repeat customers, pricing power.

FINAL WORD: DON'T WAIT TO BE PROVEN — BECOME BELIEVABLE NOW

You don't need to be an industry giant to look legitimate. You need to look competent. Composed. Ready. That's how trust is built in the early days. That's how you go from being a stranger to becoming a household name.

Machiavelli didn't offer feel-good wisdom. He gave survival strategy. You're not on Amazon to play it safe. You're here to win. And the path to winning, especially as a new seller, starts with mastering perception, earning trust through results, and acting like the brand you intend to become — not the one you are today.

You are a new prince in a crowded empire. Take the throne like you mean it.

Chapter 3: On Fortune and Timing (The Algorithm and You)

"Fortune is a woman, and if you want to control her, you must treat her roughly."
— Niccolò Machiavelli, *The Prince*

Machiavelli's take on fortune is brutal, clear, and surprisingly applicable to modern business. He believed fortune — luck, timing, opportunity — plays a role in every outcome. But he also believed that waiting passively for good fortune is a losing game. Fortune rewards the bold, not the cautious. Those who sit still get crushed by the tides. Those who act — forcefully, decisively, and at the right moment — seize advantage.

When Machiavelli called fortune a woman, he wasn't being poetic — he was being tactical. He saw fortune as something wild and unpredictable, but also something that could be influenced, guided, even bent to one's will with enough courage and preparation. To Machiavelli, power comes to those who pursue it with aggression and timing. Those who hesitate get nothing.

Now, drop that idea into the Amazon marketplace.

Amazon is ruled not by a king or a council, but by an algorithm. It is Fortuna, reborn in code. It controls what customers see. It determines who gets the Buy Box, who gets buried, who gets reviews shown, who gets punished. And just like the fortune Machiavelli wrote about, Amazon's algorithm is opaque, capricious, and ever-shifting. You can't predict it perfectly, but you can learn to play it.

To survive here, you must stop thinking of the algorithm as some neutral machine. Start thinking of it as a living force — a chaotic but influenceable power that rewards boldness, punishes indecision, and ignores those who fail to act fast.

This chapter is about hacking timing, reading the signals of the algorithm, and mastering speed as a weapon. Just as Machiavelli advised rulers to act before their enemies could respond, so too must Amazon sellers learn to strike at the right moment, launch at the right time, and move with speed that others can't match.

FORTUNE FAVORS THE BOLD — AND THE PREPARED

"Fortune shows her power where valor has not prepared to resist her," Machiavelli said. What does that mean for you? It means sellers who don't prepare — who launch without a strategy, who don't study the calendar, who ignore data — get crushed by those who do.

Let's say you're launching a product. You've got great packaging, a solid supplier, decent pricing. But you decide to list it in the middle of a slow season, without enough reviews, and with no ad budget. You're hoping something will "catch."

That's not valor. That's wishful thinking.

Now imagine the opposite. You've mapped seasonal demand. You know search volume spikes in late October. You've gathered 10 Vine reviews before launch. You've got lightning-fast FBA inventory placement, and a full ad campaign ready to go on launch day. When the market heats up, you don't react — you *strike*.

That's preparation. That's boldness. That's what Machiavelli would call commanding fortune instead of serving it.

THE ALGORITHM AS FORTUNA

Amazon's algorithm is not static. It is not logical in the way sellers wish it was. It responds to velocity, conversion rate, click-through rate, price fluctuations, stockouts, review timing, return behavior, and more — all in real time. It's a swirling machine of behavioral data and customer intent. You can't control it directly. But you can influence it.

The algorithm rewards momentum. It boosts listings that generate sales quickly. It favors products that get consistent reviews. It observes how long people stay on your listing, how often they buy after clicking, and how fast you respond to buyer concerns. It is constantly scanning for patterns that signal: *this product is relevant, trusted, and in demand.*

That means you're not just selling to customers. You're selling to an algorithm.

And like Machiavelli's Fortuna, the algorithm rewards those who move with confident aggression. Hesitate, and someone else will occupy the space you're aiming for. Launch weak, and you may never recover. Wait too long to respond to a trend, and by the time you act, the opportunity is gone.

This is the dance of timing. You don't wait for the perfect moment. You **create** it — with planning, precision, and speed.

HACKING TIMING: SEASONALITY, LAUNCH WINDOWS, REVIEW VELOCITY

Let's talk tactics.

1. Seasonal Relevance

Some products live and die by season. Selling ski gloves? You've got a window from late October to early February. Wait until December to launch and you've already missed the climb. Selling beach umbrellas? Don't drop your listing in August.

Use historical data. Google Trends. Helium10. Look for when searches begin to rise — not when they peak. Launch right as interest begins to build. That's your wave. You ride the surge instead of paddling into whitewater with no traction.

Machiavelli's princes who waited for certainty were always outmaneuvered by those who acted before the terrain hardened. The same is true here. Be early. Be prepared. Let others play catch-up.

2. Product Launch Windows

A launch window isn't just about calendar timing — it's about marketplace conditions.

- Are your competitors out of stock?

- Are prices temporarily inflated?

- Has a major player exited the category?

- Is there a social trend pushing demand?

These are your moments.

Fortune in Amazon often looks like this: a competitor with 5,000 reviews suddenly goes out of stock. Their loyal customers go hunting. If your product is ready — optimized listing, smart pricing, solid visuals — you can catch a percentage of their traffic and convert. You don't need to be better. You need to be **available** and **visible** at the right time.

3. Review Velocity

The algorithm doesn't just care how many reviews you have. It cares how **fast** you're getting them. A sudden spike in reviews suggests buzz, momentum, relevance. A trickle suggests indifference. You want the former.

So build systems for early review capture. Use Vine. Use inserts. Build email flows (compliant with TOS). Push external traffic that converts well. The goal is not just reviews — it's **fast** reviews, within the first 30 days of launch.

If you delay review collection, you delay trust. And delay, in Machiavellian terms, is death. "Delay always breeds danger," he wrote, and on Amazon, slow sellers rarely get a second chance.

INVESTING IN SPEED

Speed is your sword. If you move faster than the market, you win. If you move slower, you die.

Every part of your business must be optimized for velocity:

1. Fast Inventory Turnover

Dead stock is dead power. Amazon tracks sell-through rates. It tracks how long your product sits. Slow-moving inventory costs you in storage fees, ranking, and momentum.

Set up inventory planning that matches your sales forecasts — not your hopes. Run lean. Replenish often. Machiavelli's prince always maintained a well-supplied army. Your inventory is your army. Don't leave it stranded.

Use tools to monitor sales pace and adjust purchase orders dynamically. Forecast with realism. Avoid the rookie mistake of buying 10,000 units of a product that's unproven.

2. Fast Customer Response

Amazon cares how fast you respond to buyers. So do customers. If you leave a message unanswered for two days, your chances of a negative review skyrocket. Your seller metrics take a hit. Your account gets flagged.

Automate where you can. Set up templates. Train VAs if you're scaling. Build a reputation as a seller who answers quickly, fixes issues, and takes care of buyers. It pays off in repeat business and algorithmic trust.

Machiavelli's successful prince was always *alert*. He didn't sit in the palace and hope problems resolved themselves. He acted. So should you.

3. Fast Decisions

Analysis paralysis is a killer. Yes, data matters. But once you have 70% clarity, move. Waiting for perfect information is a fantasy. By the time you're "sure," your competitor already launched, ranked, and dominated.

Make fast calls on:

- Pausing or scaling ads

- Killing underperforming SKUs

- Adjusting pricing

- Tweaking titles or images

You can always course-correct. But you can't get back lost time. As Machiavelli said, "Tardiness often robs us opportunity."

TIMING AND DOMINANCE: A CASE FOR ATTACK

Let's connect everything: Fortune, timing, speed, and power.

Machiavelli believed that rulers who waited too long to act lost the chance to shape events. Once a crisis is mature, it's already too late to prevent it. The same applies to opportunity on Amazon. Once a trend is obvious, it's over. The sellers who made money were the ones who acted when it was *unclear*, when others hesitated.

Being bold doesn't mean being reckless. It means having a bias toward action, a culture of speed, and the systems in place to execute quickly when the opportunity appears.

And when it does — when you see a competitor stumble, when a market shifts, when demand spikes — don't walk. **Run.**

Adjust your pricing. Launch your ad campaign. Fire up external traffic. Send an email blast. Drop a TikTok. Get reviews flowing. Reinforce your ranking.

Fortune doesn't wait.

FINAL STRATEGIC TRUTHS

1. **Amazon's algorithm is your arena. Learn it, feed it, influence it.**

2. **Speed is not just helpful — it is strategic power.**

3. **Launches must be timed with precision, not guesswork.**

4. **Momentum is everything. Build it, protect it, scale it.**

5. **Act boldly, or not at all.**

You don't win on Amazon by hoping for good fortune. You win by acting like it owes you something — and then working every angle until you make that fortune your reality.

Machiavelli wouldn't have survived as an Amazon seller by being cautious. He would've tracked seasonality, studied the algorithm, used every leverage point at his disposal, and moved fast when the door opened. Not with fear. But with focus.

Amazon rewards the prince who doesn't just wait for luck — but builds his empire on top of it.

Chapter 4: Maintain Power with Results (Rank, Sales, Reviews)

"The first method for estimating the intelligence of a ruler is to look at the men he has around him."
— Niccolò Machiavelli, *The Prince*

Once you've claimed your ground in the Amazon marketplace—once you've launched your product, built some initial traction, and started to look like a serious player—you've entered a new phase of the war: holding what you've taken.

This is where most sellers begin to drift. They get comfortable. They assume the algorithm will keep rewarding them. They stop evolving their listing. They delay responses. They relax their pricing strategy. And before they even realize it, someone faster, sharper, and hungrier comes along and starts peeling away their market share.

Machiavelli would've called it weakness of rule. Because power, once gained, must be actively **maintained**. It isn't static. It's alive, and it's constantly under threat—from new rivals, changing buyer behavior, and the unpredictable shifts of the algorithm. And Machiavelli knew the truth modern Amazon sellers need to tattoo on their strategy: **results are everything**.

In a world ruled by performance metrics, visibility algorithms, and customer sentiment, your rank, sales velocity, and review score *are* your crown jewels. Lose control of them, and you lose your seat. Manage them ruthlessly, and you become untouchable.

This chapter is about what it means to rule like a serious seller—not just during a product launch, but every day after. It's about building systems, choosing your court wisely, and treating your metrics not as numbers on a dashboard, but as the lifeblood of your reign.

YOUR COURT: TOOLS, PARTNERS, SYSTEMS

Machiavelli judged the intelligence of a ruler by looking at the people he surrounded himself with. Was the prince wise enough to pick capable, loyal, and strategic advisors—or did he rely on flatterers, opportunists, and fools?

For Amazon sellers, the equivalent is your **toolset, your partners, and your systems**. These aren't just background components—they're active parts of your daily ability to make decisions, execute quickly, and stay on top.

Let's break this down:

Tools

Your tools are your spies, your scouts, and your statisticians. Tools like Helium10, Jungle Scout, Keepa, and Sellerboard are not optional. They are essential to understanding your kingdom.

- They show you keyword movement.

- They reveal competitor trends.

- They help monitor profitability.

- They alert you to changes in ranking, pricing, or Buy Box status.

A ruler without intelligence is a fool waiting to be outmaneuvered. A seller without data is a brand waiting to be crushed.

Machiavelli wrote: *"The prince must always read history, and reflect upon the actions of great men to learn from them."* In modern terms, the history and actions of others are visible in the data. If you're not watching it, someone else is—about you.

Partners

Suppliers. Freight forwarders. Virtual assistants. Photographers. Graphic designers. PPC managers. Your business is only as strong as the people you bring into your court.

Choose them as Machiavelli would: not for friendship, not for loyalty alone, but for **effectiveness**.

If your freight forwarder delivers late, it costs you rank. If your PPC manager overspends, it eats your margin. If your VA makes listing errors, it triggers customer complaints and possibly suspensions.

You must hold your partners to a high standard. And just like Machiavelli's ideal prince, you must be willing to remove anyone who underperforms—**fast**.

You are building an empire. There's no room for weak links.

Systems

The modern prince runs on **SOPs**—standard operating procedures. Repeatable, efficient, optimized processes that allow for consistency and scale.

Your SOPs are the unseen infrastructure that makes your kingdom run. From product research to customer service replies, you need defined workflows. These systems reduce mistakes. They train your people. They free your attention.

Machiavelli wrote: *"The main foundations of all states... are good laws and good arms."* Your laws are your systems. Your arms are your tools and staff. You need both.

THE THREE METRICS THAT DEFINE YOUR POWER

Now let's talk numbers. Because Machiavelli was not a dreamer. He didn't believe in theory or hope. He believed in *measurable outcomes*.

As an Amazon seller, your power exists in three metrics:

1. **Rank**

2. **Review Score**

3. **Conversion Rate**

Control these three, and you control the arena.

Rank

Ranking on Amazon is everything. If you're not on page one, you're invisible. If you're at the top of page one, you're printing money.

Machiavelli said: *"A wise prince ought to adopt such a course that his citizens will always in every sort and kind of circumstance have need of his government."* In Amazon terms, that means putting your product in front of buyers consistently—being visible and indispensable.

Ranking is based on sales velocity, conversion, keyword relevance, and review momentum. To stay ranked, you must constantly manage:

- Keyword performance: Are you indexing and converting?

- PPC strategy: Are you defending your top terms with sponsored placements?

- Pricing: Are you competitive without bleeding margin?

- Stock: Are you avoiding stockouts or long lead times?

If any of these slip, so does your rank. And once you fall, climbing back up is harder every time.

You must treat your position on the digital shelf like a fortress. Watch it. Guard it. Defend it with ads, content updates, and timely adjustments.

Review Score

Your review score isn't just social proof. It's **trust capital**. A drop from 4.6 to 4.3 can tank conversion, especially in high-competition categories.

Machiavelli said: *"It is not titles that honor men, but men that honor titles."* Your five-star rating means nothing if it's not maintained. You need real reviews from real buyers—consistently, and in volume.

Manage your review score like a reputation:

- Monitor negative reviews daily.

- Respond publicly when appropriate.

- Implement feedback quickly (fix defects, improve packaging, tweak instructions).

- Use insert cards to request feedback and deflect complaints before they become public.

And remember: silence is dangerous. If you're not actively managing reviews, you're letting your enemies write your legacy.

Conversion Rate

You can have all the traffic in the world, but if your listing doesn't convert, it's wasted.

Machiavelli wrote: *"A prince must imitate the fox and the lion, for the lion cannot protect himself from traps, and the fox cannot defend himself from wolves."*

The fox is your strategy—your copy, your storytelling, your branding. The lion is your raw strength—your pricing, your review count, your shipping time. Together, they convert browsers into buyers.

Track your conversion rate obsessively. Optimize:

- Main image (does it pop?)

- Secondary images (do they show value?)

- A+ content (does it build trust?)

- Price (does it reflect quality without scaring buyers?)

- Title and bullets (are they clear and benefit-driven?)

Conversion rate is your moat. The higher it is, the more efficient your ads become, the faster you rank, the more reviews you earn.

MANAGING KPIs LIKE A PRINCE MANAGES A KINGDOM

Your KPIs—key performance indicators—are not just business metrics. They are **territory markers**. Each one tells you if your kingdom is growing, stable, or under siege.

Machiavelli advised rulers to inspect their lands, understand their people, anticipate rebellion, and strengthen borders. Apply that directly:

- **Daily:** Check your ranking, sales, ad spend, customer messages.

- **Weekly:** Review keyword performance, inventory levels, review velocity.

- **Monthly:** Analyze ROI, profit margins, category changes, competitor moves.

If you're not managing these like a hawk, you're not ruling—you're hoping.

And hope is not a strategy.

Each KPI needs ownership. Someone in your business—maybe it's just you at first—must be responsible for watching and acting on these numbers. Because problems don't announce themselves. They show up quietly—slipping rank, slower sales, longer lead times. If you're not watching, they can grow into disasters.

Machiavelli said: *"It is much more secure to be feared than to be loved, when one has to choose."* Be feared by your competitors not because you're loud—but because you're **disciplined**.

Because your numbers are dialed in. Because you move fast when the data shifts.

WHAT HAPPENS WHEN YOU SLIP?

Let's be real.

Every kingdom experiences pressure. Competitors attack. Buyers complain. The algorithm changes. Your stock arrives late. Your ad campaign underperforms. What you do next matters more than what just happened.

Machiavelli didn't write *The Prince* as a guide to avoid failure. He wrote it to show how to recover from it—and use it.

If your review score drops, **invest in fixes**—improve the product, overhaul your listing, reach out to customers who left poor feedback. Own the issue and solve it.

If your rank falls, **audit your listing**—have keywords shifted? Is your click-through rate dropping? Are your ads underfunded? Attack the problem surgically.

If conversion tanks, **split test** everything. Images. Titles. Bullets. Offers. Price points. Then move fast on the data.

Machiavelli would say: *"The wise man does at once what the fool does finally."*

Never wait to fix a problem. Fix it now, or you'll pay ten times the price later.

FINAL WORD: RESULTS ARE YOUR REIGN

Forget what you think makes a "good" seller. Forget passion. Forget vision. Forget intention.

Results keep you in power.

Every day, the algorithm measures you. Buyers judge you. Competitors test you. And your KPIs reflect it all.

There is no hiding. There is no coasting.

You are a prince in a cutthroat digital empire. You don't get to rest on your launch. You don't get rewarded for effort. You get rewarded for outcomes—rank, sales, reviews.

Control them, and you write the future of your brand. Lose control, and you become just another failed ruler in the graveyard of abandoned ASINs.

Machiavelli understood that power wasn't just about gaining position—it was about **maintaining it with discipline, strategy, and fearlessness.**

Rule your data like a prince. Or prepare to be replaced by one who will.

Chapter 5: Fear, Love, and the Buy Box

"It is much safer to be feared than loved, if one must choose."
— Niccolò Machiavelli, *The Prince*

In the eyes of a customer, there is only one true owner of a product listing on Amazon: the seller who holds the Buy Box.

The Buy Box is the gatekeeper of sales. It decides who makes money and who watches from the sidelines. On any given product page, dozens of sellers may exist behind the scenes, but only one sits on the throne. Only one gets the customer's click by default. Only one is the "chosen one" in the eyes of the algorithm.

That seller is the one who controls the Buy Box.

Getting the Buy Box—and keeping it—is not a matter of luck. It's a brutal, calculated fight. It requires speed, precision, data, customer obsession, and sometimes, war. It's a battlefield where Machiavelli's principles apply with stunning clarity. Holding power, earning loyalty, managing perception, deploying force when needed—all of it comes into play when you're fighting for that single piece of digital real estate.

This chapter is about how the Buy Box functions as a crown of legitimacy. It's about the tools of fear, the tools of love, and how to balance both without collapsing your brand's perceived value. Because in the world of Amazon, you must learn to dominate through strategy—not just to be liked, but to be *chosen*.

THE BUY BOX: DIGITAL CROWN, ALGORITHMIC THRONE

To understand the fight for the Buy Box, you must first grasp what it represents.

The Buy Box is not a visual trophy. It's a dynamic, algorithm-driven decision made by Amazon based on multiple performance factors: price, shipping time, stock levels, feedback rating, seller history, fulfillment method, and more. When a customer clicks "Add to Cart" or "Buy Now," the order goes to the seller who currently "owns" the Buy Box—even if multiple sellers are offering the same product.

So whether you're reselling another brand's item or controlling your own private label listing, the Buy Box defines whether you're in the game or just watching from the sidelines.

Holding the Buy Box is like sitting on a throne with a hundred daggers pointed at you. You're in charge—for now. But someone always wants your seat. The algorithm is constantly reviewing every seller's performance. The second you slip—your price rises, your delivery time increases, your customer service drops—you can be dethroned.

Machiavelli would have seen the Buy Box as the ultimate test of rule. Power must be earned through results, not promises. It must be defended daily. And above all, it must serve the people—or they will turn on you.

FEAR: THE DARK ART OF BUY BOX CONTROL

In *The Prince*, Machiavelli famously said it is safer to be feared than loved. He didn't mean cruelty for its own sake. He meant that fear—when properly directed—creates stability. Fear makes enemies think twice. Fear keeps rivals in check.

On Amazon, "fear" takes the form of competitive pressure: **automated repricers, legal enforcement, and market retaliation.**

1. Price Suppression via Automated Repricers

When multiple sellers compete for the same listing, price wars break out. Repricers scan the marketplace and automatically adjust your price to stay competitive, sometimes updating multiple times per hour. You set the rules—minimum price, maximum price, aggressiveness—and let the machine go to war for you.

This can be devastating.

Sellers who don't use repricers are immediately outgunned. And even those who do can quickly spiral into price suppression where profit disappears and the Buy Box becomes a race to the bottom.

Still, when used strategically, repricers **create fear**. They force other sellers into reactive positions. You can maintain control by being aggressive, fast, and smart in your repricing logic. You can set traps—drop the price temporarily, then raise it once competitors fall out. You can hold price lines in coordination with stock manipulation, forcing others into high-inventory losses.

Machiavelli said: *"Men are driven by two principal impulses, either by love or by fear."* In the Buy Box, fear often means price pressure. The seller who can hold the line longest usually wins—but only if they do so with purpose.

2. Legal and Tactical Retaliation

Another fear tactic is legal enforcement. If you're a brand owner, you can use intellectual property protection, cease-and-desist letters, and Amazon's infringement systems to **remove hijackers**—those who jump onto your listing and attempt to steal sales.

The most effective Amazon sellers don't allow leeches to hang on. They document violations, enforce trademarks, and get serious about protecting their turf.

This creates a chilling effect. If hijackers know your brand is aggressive, they'll think twice before jumping on your listing. If you allow them to exist without pushback, you invite more. As Machiavelli advised: *"Injuries must be inflicted all at once... so that being tasted less, they offend less."* Strike quickly and decisively.

You can also use tactical maneuvers like **stock monitoring**, **review analysis**, and **competitive mapping** to predict and counter your rivals' movements. Show them you're watching. Respond quickly to their actions. Don't wait to be attacked—**neutralize threats before they mature**.

LOVE: CUSTOMER OBSESSION AND BUY BOX FAVOR

If fear keeps competitors at bay, love keeps customers close—and keeps Amazon's algorithm favoring you.

Amazon's entire business model is based on customer obsession. So if you want the Buy Box, you must play by Amazon's highest rule: **serve the customer better than anyone else.**

This means optimizing every inch of your experience, from listing to logistics.

1. Optimized Listings That Convert

The algorithm doesn't just look at price. It watches conversion rate. If 100 people click your listing and 35 buy, and your competitor only converts 25, you will win the Buy Box—even at a higher price.

So your listing needs to perform. Your images must be sharp. Your title must hook. Your bullet points must deliver clarity and confidence. Your A+ content must reinforce trust.

Machiavelli wrote: *"Men in general judge more by the eye than by the hand... because everyone sees you, but few come in touch with you."* This is a perfect metaphor for listing optimization. The buyer doesn't know you personally. They don't touch your product until after they purchase. Their entire judgment is based on perception—your photos, your reviews, your promises.

So make it count. This is where "love" is earned—not by being soft, but by being excellent.

2. Customer Service that Creates Loyalty

Your post-sale behavior matters too.

- Do you respond to messages within hours, not days?

- Do you solve problems proactively?

- Do you offer refunds with grace?

- Do you track and resolve negative feedback?

If so, Amazon notices. Your Order Defect Rate stays low. Your Seller Rating climbs. Your buyers leave better reviews.

And the Buy Box algorithm rewards this. Because Amazon wants its customers to come back. And they only do that when the sellers make it easy, fast, and satisfying.

Think like Machiavelli here. Love isn't about pleasing everyone. It's about earning stability. You build customer affection not with charm, but with competence. You become their trusted seller. Their reliable merchant. Their go-to.

This is **power through consistency**.

3. Product Quality and Packaging

None of the above matters if your product is junk.

If customers are consistently disappointed, the algorithm will notice. You'll rack up returns. Negative reviews. Complaints. Account flags. And you'll be removed from the Buy Box—even if you're the only seller on the listing.

"Love" here means exceeding expectations. A product that does what it claims to do, arrives faster than promised, and looks better in person than in the photos. This creates fans. It also creates positive seller feedback, which is still a Buy Box signal, especially in FBM (Fulfilled By Merchant) setups.

Quality is your long game. Love is built through reliability. Buyers come back to what they trust.

THE BALANCE: PRICE AGGRESSION WITHOUT DESTROYING VALUE

This is where many sellers fail.

They confuse aggression with recklessness. They slash prices to win the Buy Box, only to destroy their brand's value. They race to the bottom, then wonder why their profit is gone, their reviews are sour, and no one respects their product.

Machiavelli warned against this. *"A prince who is despised is of so little account that he is not feared by any one."* That's exactly what happens when you price too low for too long. You're not feared. You're not loved. You're disposable.

The smart seller knows when to push, when to pull, and how to keep value perception high even while competing on price.

Tactics for Maintaining Balance:

- **Strategic Promotions**: Use Lightning Deals, coupons, and limited-time sales to create urgency without permanently damaging price expectations.

- **Bundle Pricing**: Offer value-adds (free accessories, digital guides, multi-packs) to justify higher price points while holding the Buy Box.

- **Time-Based Repricing**: Drop price temporarily to secure the Buy Box, then raise once ranking and velocity improve.

- **Anchor Pricing**: Show a higher "list price" to establish value, then use your actual price to create the appearance of a deal.

The goal is this: **look affordable without looking cheap**. That's the art. That's the balance between fear and love. You want competitors to fear your efficiency and customers to love your value.

You want the algorithm to see you as *the logical choice*—the best offer at this moment in time.

REIGNING FROM THE BUY BOX

When you control the Buy Box consistently, you do more than just make sales. You **own** the customer experience.

You shape their first impression of the product. You collect the reviews. You get the cross-sell and upsell opportunities. You become the brand of record—even if other sellers are present in the background.

This gives you leverage:

- You can launch variations more easily.

- You can test pricing without losing traffic.

- You can collect better data and optimize accordingly.

- You become the default seller, which compounds trust and visibility.

Machiavelli spoke of the strength of dynasties. Once a prince becomes loved by the people and feared by his enemies, he can rule for decades. The same holds true in the Buy Box. When you've earned both customer loyalty and competitive dominance, your position becomes self-reinforcing.

But it is **never safe**. You must monitor your metrics daily. You must stay vigilant. You must remain paranoid.

Because the Buy Box doesn't care about your history. It cares about your current performance. If you slip, it will hand your crown to someone else.

And if you're not ready to fight to keep it, you were never fit to rule.

FINAL WORD: LOVE, FEAR, AND ALGORITHMIC POWER

You cannot win the Buy Box with kindness alone. Nor can you hold it with aggression alone. You need both.

Fear keeps competitors away. Love keeps customers loyal. Balance them wisely. Use automation, data, and legal tools to enforce your rule. Use branding, service, and quality to inspire trust.

Above all, act like a ruler who knows the game—and refuses to surrender the throne.

Because on Amazon, there is no democracy. There is only the Buy Box. And there can be only one king at a time.

Chapter 6: Destroy or Be Destroyed (Dealing with Competitors)

"In taking a state, the new ruler must extinguish the family of the old prince."
— Niccolò Machiavelli, *The Prince*

In Machiavelli's ruthless world, there is no middle ground. When a prince seizes power, he must eliminate any possibility of resurgence by the previous dynasty. The logic is simple: as long as the old family lives, plots and rebellions can be hatched. Transposed to Amazon selling, this brutal lesson translates into one unyielding principle: **to secure your turf, you must neutralize every threat**. Competitors who nibble away at your Buy Box share, hijack your listings, or siphon off your customers can never be tolerated. You must outlast them, outmaneuver them, or eliminate them altogether.

This chapter shows you how to wage total war on your rivals—and how to protect your throne once you've seized it. We'll examine four core strategies:

1. **Hijacker Defense**

2. **Branding Moats**

3. **External Traffic Leverage**

4. **Legal Options (IP Claims, MAP Enforcement)**

Each of these tactics, wielded skillfully, arms you for the inevitable fights that arise on Amazon. Ignore them, and your empire will crumble.

---

1. Hijacker Defense: Protecting Your Listings from Invaders

Imagine you've built a pristine castle—stellar reviews, polished listings, a flawless track record—and then you wake up one morning to discover squatters on your land. That's what happens when hijackers latch onto your listing: they piggyback on your reviews, undercut your price, and shred your conversion rate. Machiavelli's injunction to "extinguish the family of the old prince" is apropos: you must root out these opportunists at the first sign of infestation.

Early Detection

The first step is vigilance. Hijackers often appear quietly: a new offer pops up, priced a few cents below yours. To detect them:

- **Automated Monitoring Tools**
  Set up alerts in tools like Sellerboard or Helium10 to notify you whenever your ASIN's Buy Box or offer panel changes.

- **Daily Audits**
  Make it a habit to check your listing multiple times per day, especially during peak sales hours, to ensure no rogue

offers have appeared.

- **Third-Party Surveillance**
  Services like Tracktor can watch your ASIN and send email or SMS alerts when hijackers emerge.

Once detected, immediate action is required. Time is your enemy: every minute a hijacker remains reduces your Buy Box percentage and dents your brand's reputation.

Immediate Countermeasures

- **Price Matching (Temporarily)**
  If the hijacker is undercutting by pennies, match their price to wrest control of the Buy Box while other defenses mobilize.

- **Suppress Unauthorized SKUs**
  Report the rogue offer to Amazon as "unauthorized seller" if you have Brand Registry. In many cases, Amazon will remove the offer within hours.

- **Inventory Manipulation**
  If you're using Fulfillment By Merchant (FBM), temporarily remove your SKU and relist it to purge the hijacker's SKU, then re-enable your own. Do **not** do this frequently, or you risk algorithmic penalties.

Long-Term Defense

- **Brand Registry & Project Zero**
  Enroll in Amazon Brand Registry to gain tools like Project Zero's self-service takedown of counterfeit or unauthorized listings.

- **Transparent Packaging and Serialization**
  Use unique packaging and serialized barcodes that Amazon's frustration-free packaging service can verify, making it harder for hijackers to counterfeit or resell generic stock.

- **Authorized Reseller Networks**
  Limit your distribution to vetted partners. By reducing the avenues through which hijackers can source your product, you choke off their supply.

Machiavelli would nod approvingly: strike swiftly, make an example of them, and discourage any further attempts. A reputation for ruthless defense deters would-be invaders.

---

2. Branding Moats: Fortifying Your Empire Beyond Price Wars

Price competition is a zero-sum game; every cent you shave off your margin only emboldens the next seller to undercut you further. Instead of relying on price alone, you need **branding**

moats—distinctive, defensible advantages that keep competitors at bay.

Define a Unique Value Proposition

- **Niche Specialization**
  Carve out a subcategory where you can be the undisputed leader. For example, instead of "yoga mats," own "eco-friendly travel yoga mats."

- **Proprietary Formulations or Designs**
  Develop features unique to your product—antimicrobial fabrics, patented locking mechanisms, or custom blends—that competitors cannot replicate immediately.

Strengthen Your Brand Identity

- **Premium Packaging and Unboxing Experience**
  A memorable first impression reinforces perceived quality. Color-coded tissue paper, custom inserts with your brand story, and a QR code linking to tutorial videos all deepen customer affinity.

- **Consistent Brand Voice**
  From your A+ Content to customer support emails, maintain a consistent tone and aesthetic that signals professionalism and builds trust.

Leverage Brand Analytics

- **Brand Dashboard Insights**
  Use Amazon's Brand Analytics (available to Brand Registered sellers) to identify top-performing search terms and buyer demographics, then tailor new products or marketing to these insights.

- **Repeat Purchase Tracking**
  Monitor who buys again and when. If you spot patterns—say, customers rebuy every 60 days—build subscription or replenishment bundles that lock them in.

Build Community

- **Loyalty Programs and Newsletters**
  Collect customer emails off Amazon via insert cards that offer special discounts or insider access. Send tailored content that fosters a sense of belonging.

- **Social Proof Beyond Amazon**
  A dedicated Instagram community or a private Facebook group for product owners creates an ecosystem where your brand thrives, and competitors can't easily intrude.

Machiavelli's ideal prince didn't rely on mercenaries—he built citizen armies. Similarly, your brand moat rests on genuine loyalty, not transient price cuts.

---

3. External Traffic Leverage: Controlling the Flow of Customers

If you depend solely on Amazon's organic search and advertising to fill your coffers, you remain at the mercy of algorithm changes and rising ad costs. The smart merchant builds independent channels—**external traffic pipelines**—to drive demand directly to their listings.

Paid Advertising Off-Amazon

- **Google Search & Shopping Ads**
  Target high-intent keywords that lead shoppers to your Amazon detail page or a custom landing page that funnels them back to Amazon for purchase and review.

- **Social Media Ads**
  Platforms like Facebook, Instagram, and TikTok let you zero in on lookalike audiences of your best customers. Use engaging video demos to capture attention, then link directly to your Amazon listing.

Owned Traffic Channels

- **Email Marketing Lists**
  Incentivize buyers to sign up post-purchase for restock reminders, new product alerts, or VIP discounts. When you launch a new variant, your list becomes day-one sales and review velocity.

- **Content Marketing and SEO**
  A blog or YouTube channel that answers customer questions about your niche positions you as an authority. Articles like "5 Ways to Extend the Life of Your Travel Yoga Mat" can rank on Google and funnel readers to your product.

Influencer Partnerships

- **Micro-Influencers**
  Partner with niche influencers whose followers trust their recommendations. A single Instagram Story swipe-up or TikTok unboxing can spark a surge in sales that the Buy Box algorithm will notice.

- **Affiliate Programs**
  Offer a cut of every sale through affiliate networks. This turns bloggers and reviewers into volunteer salespeople, expanding your reach exponentially.

The Feedback Loop to Amazon

When you successfully drive high-converting external traffic, Amazon rewards you:

1. **Burst of Sales**
   Quick influx of units sold signals relevance.

2. **Review Velocity**
   Incentivized buyers are more likely to review positively.

3. **Improved Organic Ranking**
   The algorithm elevates your ASIN for high-converting keywords.

In Machiavelli's terms, you don't just sit in your castle waiting for subjects to arrive—you send out heralds and banners, turning the tide in your favor.

---

4. Legal Options: Securing Your Rights and Enforcing Fair Play

When subtle pressures fail, it's time to wield formal authority: your legal rights. Machiavelli championed the rule of law as a tool of power: once a prince establishes clear rules and enforces them, challengers hesitate.

Intellectual Property (IP) Claims

- **Trademark Protection**
  Register your brand name and logo. Once you've got your registration number, you can file infringement notices against sellers misusing your trademark.

- **Patent Enforcement**
  If you have a genuine invention, obtain a utility or design

patent. Amazon's Brand Registry can then expedite the removal of listing violators.

- **Copyright Takedowns**
  For product images, designs, and written content, enforce your copyright to remove copied listings.

Minimum Advertised Price (MAP) Policies

- **Establish a MAP Policy**
  Draft clear rules that your authorized resellers must follow. State the minimum price at which they can advertise your product.

- **Enforce Aggressively**
  Monitor your channel partners. If a reseller violates your MAP, issue warnings, then revoke privileges. Publicize your enforcement policy on your wholesale portal to deter future violations.

Contracts and Distributor Agreements

- **Selective Distribution**
  Use contracts that limit where and how resellers can sell your products. This prevents rogue sellers from sourcing through grey-market channels.

- **Territorial Restrictions**
  In your distributor agreements, stipulate which regions or platforms each partner can serve. Violations can be

pursued legally.

Working with Amazon's Enforcement Teams

- **Brand Registry's Project Zero**
  Automatically remove suspected counterfeit listings. Use machine learning triggers and manual submissions to keep your catalog clean.

- **Transparency by Amazon**
  Enroll your products in Amazon's serialization service. Each unit gets a unique code, making it easier to identify and remove counterfeits or unauthorized units.

Machiavelli would approve: set the laws, make them clear, and enforce them without hesitation. Competitors who know you'll take them to Amazon's enforcement channels—or to court—will think twice before testing your defenses.

Bringing It All Together: A Unified Strategy of Dominance

Each of these strategies—hijacker defense, branding moats, external traffic leverage, and legal enforcement—represents a pillar of your competitive fortress. Alone, they offer partial protection. Together, they form an impenetrable stronghold.

1. **Detect and Purge**
    Use vigilant monitoring and swift takedowns to eliminate hijackers.

2. **Fortify Your Walls**
    Build brand loyalty and unique value that competitors can't replicate overnight.

3. **Control the Water Supply**
    Drive external traffic to maintain a steady flow of buyers, reducing reliance on Amazon's internal channels.

4. **Write and Enforce the Laws**
    Use trademarks, patents, and MAP policies to codify your rights—and enforce them ruthlessly.

In Machiavellian fashion, there is no compromise. Every moment you delay in pursuing these strategies is a moment your competitors gain ground. Every loophole you leave open is an invitation for challengers. Every day you neglect your legal rights is a gift to hijackers and counterfeiters.

Remember Machiavelli's stark warning: if you allow the old prince's family to survive, they will one day return. On Amazon, that family might be a resurgent rival brand, a savvy arbitrageur, or a counterfeit ring. Your duty as the new prince is clear: **destroy or be destroyed**.

When you master these tactics, you do more than defend your listing—you establish a legacy. You become the merchant to beat. You turn your launch into a dynasty.

Your competitors will test you. They will probe for weaknesses, attack when you're distracted, and exploit every gap they find. Show them none. Wield these strategies with precision and ruthlessness. Leave no rival standing.

Chapter 7: Play Dirty (But Smart)

"A prince, therefore, who desires to maintain himself must learn not to be good, and to use this ability or not according to necessity."
— Niccolò Machiavelli, *The Prince*

Machiavelli's stark realism shatters any illusions that business—or politics—are governed by virtue alone. In his world, "the ends justify the means" is not a slogan but a rule: when survival and success are at stake, moral scruples give way to ruthless pragmatism. For today's Amazon seller, the same applies. There are tactics in the gray zones—ethical if wielded carefully, effective if deployed judiciously—that can tip the balance in your favor. This chapter explores how and when to "play dirty" without crossing into ruinous territory, covering four critical arenas:

1. **Review Building Strategies**

2. **Keyword "Stuffing" Within TOS Limits**

3. **Shadow ASIN Techniques**

4. **Reputation Management & Damage Control**

Each section shows how to push boundaries intelligently—always with an eye on compliance, sustainability, and long-term brand health.

I. Review Building Strategies

Machiavelli warned rulers to secure the loyalty of their people by any means necessary. On Amazon, reviews are your subjects' votes of confidence. A lack of positive reviews is vulnerability; a surge of five-star feedback is a fortress around your listing. But Amazon's rules prohibit direct incentives or manipulations. The trick is to use every legal avenue, micro-optimizing your review funnel so that "forced" love becomes organic momentum.

1. Leverage Amazon Vine with Surgical Precision

- **Selective Enrollment**
  Don't throw every SKU into Vine. Choose only your hero products—those with proven conversion potential and supply chain reliability. A well-reviewed hero ASIN raises the profile of your entire brand.

- **Post-Vine Sequencing**
  After the initial Vine reviews, follow up with a customer email flow (compliant with Amazon's Buyer-Seller Messaging Policy) thanking participants and subtly reminding them to share updated opinions once they've had real-world use.

2. Insert Cards and Packaging Prompts

- **Soft-Touch Requests**
  Include a small, beautifully designed card inside every package. The message: "We hope you love your [Product].

If you do, please consider sharing your experience on Amazon. Your feedback helps us improve."

- **Offer Support, Not Incentives**
  Emphasize that you're there to help if something's wrong—offer customer service contact info prominently. Customers who feel heard are more likely to leave positive reviews than those who feel pressured or ignored.

3. External Review Drives: Controlled Outreach

- **Email Capture for Post-Purchase Follow-Up**
  Within the bounds of Amazon's policies, direct customers to a branded landing page offering usage tips, tutorial videos, or a community link in exchange for optional email signup. Then run a timed email campaign focusing on user education first—review requests come only after value delivery.

- **Micro-Influencers & Affiliate Networks**
  Ship free units to niche bloggers and YouTubers under a clear agreement: honest review in return for product. Disclose that the review may be negative; regulators demand transparency. Many micro-influencers will nonetheless provide a balanced, often favorable write-up that generates both sales and genuine reviews.

4. Timing and Volume: Machiavellian Momentum

- **Burst Strategy**
  Aim for review spikes—20–30 reviews within the first two
  weeks of launch. A sudden volume jump signals Amazon's
  algorithm that your product is "hot," boosting organic rank
  and visibility.

- **Steady Drip for Longevity**
  After the burst, maintain a moderate but consistent pace
  of 5–10 reviews per month through continued outreach and
  customer engagement. A plateau or decline in review
  velocity can choke off long-term growth.

Throughout all of this, remember Machiavelli's counsel: *"He must
not deviate from good, if possible, but should know how to enter
into evil when forced by necessity."* If your product genuinely
delights, these tactics simply accelerate word-of-mouth; if flaws
emerge, ethical failures will surface swiftly. Always monitor ratings
and feedback sentiment—adjust or cease a campaign if quality
issues arise.

II. Keyword "Stuffing" Within TOS Limits

In *The Prince*, Machiavelli exhorts rulers to master both the lion's
force and the fox's cunning. On Amazon, the lion is your product,
the fox your keywords. Too little optimization and you're invisible;

too much, and Amazon penalizes you. The art is to target every relevant search term—without trespassing into prohibited territory.

1. Backend Keywords: Hidden Real Estate

- **Maximize Space, Minimize Redundancy**
  Combine plurals, singulars, synonyms, and alternative spellings into your backend fields. Do not repeat terms already present in title or bullets. Use every character slot without stuffing duplicates, and avoid competitor trademarks to stay within policy.

- **Localize for Key Markets**
  If you sell in multiple regions, translate terms (e.g., "jumper cables" in the U.S. vs. "booster leads" in the UK), capturing regional search habits.

2. Title & Bullet Point Strategies

- **Structured, Benefit-Driven Bullets**
  Begin each bullet with the most important keyword, but immediately pivot to a customer benefit. E.g., "Foldable Camping Chair – Ultra-light design for easy travel." This packs keywords "foldable camping chair" while leading with the feature that matters.

- **Synonym Injection**
  Where space allows, append secondary terms: "Slip-resistant grip for yoga [mat, exercise mat, Pilates mat]." Only include 2–3 brackets per bullet to avoid

bloating.

3. Image & A+ Content Keyword Etiquette

- **Text Overlays with Keywords**
  On lifestyle images, overlay a concise phrase: "Leakproof Water Bottle for Hiking." This supports your caption SEO while serving customers visually.

- **A+ Module Headings**
  Use module headings as natural keyword magnets: "Why Choose Our BPA-Free Water Bottle" instead of "Product Benefits."

4. Monitoring and Adaptation

- **Search Term Reports & Query Mining**
  Weekly, analyze Amazon Search Term Reports. Identify high-CTR, low-CPC terms not in your listing yet. Test additions in bullets or backend.

- **Negative Keyword Exclusion**
  For Sponsored Products, suppress irrelevant clicks by adding negative keywords—avoid wasting budget on off-target searches.

Machiavelli's fox would approve: cunning, flexible, and always one step ahead of the hunting dogs.

III. Shadow ASIN Strategies

"Shadow ASINs" are stealth listings—parallel or near-identical ASINs used to gather incremental share, test variants, or protect main listings from overexposure. This tactic lives firmly in the gray, requiring surgical discretion.

1. Purposeful Splintering

- **Variant Testing Without Risk**
  Launch a shadow ASIN with slightly different packaging, bundle contents, or title structure. Monitor performance for 30 days to determine which elements lift conversion. Once clear, roll the learnings into your main listing and sunset the shadow ASIN.

- **Channel Protection**
  If you sell on wholesale channels or bundles, your main ASIN may pick up unauthorized offers. Use a shadow ASIN for specialized bundles (e.g., including a bonus accessory), so your core ASIN remains pristine.

2. Traffic Diversion and Cannibalization Control

- **Controlled Cannibalization**
  If your main ASIN slows, direct select PPC or external ads to a shadow ASIN targeting long-tail keywords. This siphons marginal traffic away from the main product

without damaging its conversion metrics.

- **Sunsetting Strategy**
  After gathering insights, merge reviews via a controlled merge request, or let the shadow ASIN expire naturally—ensuring Amazon's algorithm transfers the momentum to your main listing.

3. Policy Compliance and Risk Mitigation

- **Minimal Differences**
  Ensure each shadow ASIN has genuine differences—a unique image set, a bundle component, or a regional variant. Identical duplicates risk takedown.

- **Rotating Inventory Pools**
  Use separate FNSKU labels for shadow ASINs. This isolates inventory and prevents co-mingling, which Amazon flags as abuse.

Machiavelli counseled that "he who seeks to deceive will always find someone who will allow himself to be deceived." By creating legitimate, test-purposed ASINs, you avoid the appearance of deceit while gathering strategic intelligence.

IV. Reputation Management: Damage Control When Things Backfire

Even the most careful gray-area tactics carry risk. A sudden flood of reviews might trigger Amazon's behavioral analytics; an accidental policy breach can lead to listing suspension; a misinterpreted keyword tactic can draw warnings. When missteps occur, you need a Machiavellian plan for swift, decisive damage control.

1. Monitor and Pre-empt

- **Automated Alerts**
  Use tools that flag account health metrics—Buy Box loss, sudden review removals, policy violation emails—so you can react within hours, not days.

- **Internal Penetration Testing**
  Quarterly, hire a third-party consultant or agency to audit your tactics for borderline practices. A fresh perspective spots risks your team may overlook.

2. Rapid Response Protocol

- **Apology & Correction**
  If a campaign inadvertently breaks TOS (for instance, an email template includes forbidden language), immediately pause the campaign, send a brief apology email to Amazon Seller Support, and outline your corrective

measures.

- **Data-Backed Appeals**
  In the case of a listing suspension or review purge, gather performance logs, third-party tool screenshots, and concise timelines to demonstrate compliance intent. Amazon favors sellers who present organized, factual appeals rather than emotional pleas.

3. Public Relations Within Amazon

- **Customer-Facing Acknowledgment**
  If a product defect spawns a wave of 1-star reviews, post a brief update on your A+ Content: "We've heard your feedback and have improved our design. All new units shipped after [date] feature…" This reassures new buyers and shows Amazon you're proactive in service of customers.

- **Vine Relaunch or Update**
  After product fixes, relaunch an updated unit to Vine or request Early Reviewer Program enrollment to build fresh, positive reviews that can drown out earlier negatives.

4. Long-Term Resilience

- **Continuous Quality Improvement**
  Treat every complaint as a data point. Log issues in a centralized database. Prioritize fixes in your product

roadmap.

- **Narrative Control**
  Machiavelli observed that "the vulgar crowd always is taken by appearances and by the outcome of actions." Control your narrative through your storefront: refresh your Brand Store home page with testimonials, case studies, and any awards or certifications earned. Focus customer attention on success stories, not past stumbles.

Conclusion: Calculated Ruthlessness

Perhaps Machiavelli's most unsettling lesson is that virtue alone does not secure power—**strategic ruthlessness does**. For the Amazon seller, playing dirty means stretching every rule to its limit, exploiting every crevice of algorithmic behavior, and defending your territory with both guile and force. But "dirty" does not imply reckless or unethical. Instead, it means *intelligent aggression*: pushing boundaries only where it yields genuine advantage, and retracting tactics the moment they threaten your legitimacy.

The modern prince must be a dual master: lion and fox, warrior and strategist. By employing savvy review funnels, surgical keyword optimization, shadow ASIN laboratories, and iron-clad damage control, you commandeer every tool the marketplace provides. You bend fortune to your will, not through idealism, but through **smart**, calculated action—just as Machiavelli prescribed.

Embrace the gray. Master the art. Triumph where others fail.

Chapter 8: Appear Virtuous (Even When You're Ruthless)

"Everyone sees what you appear to be, few experience what you really are."
— Niccolò Machiavelli, *The Prince*

Perception is the coin of power on Amazon. You may know, deep in your bones, every sharp tactic you've deployed to seize your slice of the marketplace. You may have cut corners, pushed rules and edged into the gray. But those behind the screens don't see your strategy—they see your storefront, your images, your copy, your customer interactions. If the public face of your brand reads as clumsy, mercenary or untrustworthy, no amount of backend wizardry will save you. The modern Machiavellian seller understands that **how you look matters far more than what you do behind the curtain**.

This chapter shows you how to wear a cloak of virtue so convincing that no buyer suspects the ruthless engine beneath. We'll explore four pillars of perceived integrity:

1. **Crafting an Impeccable Front**

2. **Polishing Every Customer Touchpoint**

3. **Leveraging Influencers and PR for Credibility**

4. **Mastering the Art of the Earnest Apology**

1. Crafting an Impeccible Front

Machiavelli advised princes to master the art of appearance: "A prince ought to inspire fear in such a way that, if he does not win love, he avoids hatred." In ecommerce terms, you need to inspire **confidence**, even if you must sacrifice comfort.

Branding That Radiates Integrity

- **Visual Consistency**: From logo to packaging to your Amazon storefront banner, every color, font and layout choice should feel cohesive and professional. A haphazard mix of styles screams "amateur."

- **Storytelling That Rings True**: Weave a concise brand narrative—your origin, mission, values—that fits naturally within A+ Content and storefront "About" pages. Speak of real challenges overcome, real benefits delivered. Avoid hyperbole. Ground your story in facts: materials sourced ethically, small-batch production, veteran-led team—details buyers can verify.

- **Transparent Policies**: Display your shipping, return and warranty policies in clear, plain language. Machiavelli said, "Men are so simple and so subject to present necessities, that he who seeks to deceive will always find someone who will allow himself to be deceived." Don't let confusion become grounds for distrust—spell out exactly how returns work, how support is accessed, and what buyers can expect.

Product Presentation That Builds Trust

- **Hero Image with Purpose**: Your primary image must be clean, on-white, with the product perfectly centered. It signals professionalism. No logos, no misleading props—just the product at its most honest.

- **Lifestyle Imagery That Resonates**: Show your product in use by real people in real settings. This conveys authenticity—buyers sense that your offering integrates seamlessly into their lives.

- **Benefit-Driven Copy**: Bullet points and descriptions should lead with what users gain ("Stays cool for 12 hours" vs. "Triple-walled construction"). Machiavelli warned against empty promises; focus on verifiable advantages.

When every element of your listing looks polished and genuine, buyers believe they're dealing with a brand that cares, even if you're employing cutthroat tactics behind the scenes.

---

2. Polishing Every Customer Touchpoint

Appearances extend beyond images and copy. Every email, every reply, every package inserted instruction is a moment to reinforce your brand's virtue.

Thoughtfully Designed Packaging

- **Unboxing as Ritual**: Include a branded thank-you card or small gift (sticker, sample) nestled inside elegant packaging. A well-executed unboxing experience feels like a gift, not just a transaction.

- **Concise Instruction Manual**: Provide clear, friendly instructions or usage tips. Customers appreciate guidance—they feel you're invested in their success, not just their purchase.

Customer Service That Feels Personal

- **Rapid, Empathetic Responses**: Craft templated replies that sound human: use the buyer's name, acknowledge their concern, and offer concrete next steps. Machiavelli urged princes to appear responsive: if you treat every message as urgent, customers believe you're fully engaged.

- **Proactive Outreach**: After a purchase, send a gentle follow-up asking if they need assistance. Position it as helpfulness rather than a review request. This not only addresses issues early (avoiding negative feedback) but cements a caring brand image.

- **Consistent Voice Across Channels**: Whether it's on Amazon messages, social media DMs or support tickets, maintain the same tone of attentive professionalism. Inconsistency signals disorganization; consistency breeds confidence.

Post-Sale Care That Converts Critics into Champions

- **Easy Returns**: Simplify the return process. A frictionless return experience leaves buyers more willing to try you again. Machiavelli noted that a clemency shown at the right time can convert enemies into allies.

- **Follow-Up Surveys**: Deploy brief, optional surveys (via email) asking how you can improve. Frame it as a desire to serve better. Even critics appreciate being heard—many soften their complaints when given a platform.

By perfecting each interaction, you create an aura of trustworthiness that endures—even when rougher tactics lurk in your operational back office.

---

3. Leveraging Influencers and PR for Credibility

No matter how polished your listing, third-party endorsements amplify perceived virtue. Machiavelli recognized the value of projecting strength through visible alliances—today, influencers and media mentions are those alliances.

Micro-Influencers: Authentic Voices

- **Strategic Selection**: Target niche influencers whose audiences match your buyer persona. A small but engaged following often yields higher trust than a celebrity with millions of followers.

- **Genuine Collaborations**: Invite influencers to co-create content—unboxing videos, how-to guides, honest demo reviews. When they showcase genuine excitement or thoughtful critique, their audience perceives your product as authentic and vetted.

Macro-Influencers and Media Outreach

- **PR Angles That Resonate**: Craft press pitches around compelling data or stories—"How a Veteran-Founded Startup Redesigns Travel Gear for Disabled Adventurers," for example. Journalists and blogs love human-interest or trend-driven hooks.

- **Third-Party Reviews**: Submit products to reputable review sites or comparison blogs. A featured review in a trusted publication translates into a halo effect for your Amazon listing—even if the user skimples it.

Social Proof Integration

- **Showcasing Endorsements**: Embed quotes or badges from influencers and media in your A+ Content. A line like,

"As seen on TravelGear.com," or "Recommended by Adventure with Alex (100K followers)," signals external validation.

- **User-Generated Content**: Encourage customers to share real photos on Instagram with a custom hashtag. Curate a feed on your brand website or storefront that highlights these images—more proof that real people love your gear.

By wrapping your brand in the glow of external advocates, you cloak your ruthless marketplace tactics in a veil of communal approval.

---

4. Mastering the Art of the Earnest Apology

No empire is flawless; mistakes happen. Machiavelli knew that a timely, strategic apology could preserve power, whereas defiance or silence invited rebellion. On Amazon, scandals might include defective batches, shipping delays, unforeseen policy suspensions, or review purges. How you respond determines whether your reputation survives unscathed.

The Four-Step Apology Framework

1. **Immediate Acknowledgment**
   As soon as an issue is identified—an influx of 1-star reviews, an account warning, a sudden defect claim—publicly (via your storefront or A+ Content) or privately (via direct email) acknowledge the problem.

"We've become aware of shipping delays affecting orders placed between June 10–12."

2. **Express Empathy**
   Show genuine understanding of customer frustration. Machiavelli extolled the value of seeming compassionate.
   "We understand how essential timely delivery is, and we are deeply sorry for the inconvenience this has caused."

3. **Outline Corrective Measures**
   Detail the concrete steps you're taking—quality control audits, new fulfillment center partnerships, free replacements, extended warranties.
   "We have added a second fulfillment partner to ensure same-day shipping, and we're conducting a 100% inspection of all outgoing units."

4. **Offer Restitution or Assurance**
   Depending on severity, provide a goodwill gesture (discount code, free accessory) or a firm guarantee.
   "As a token of our apology, all affected customers will receive a 20% voucher on their next purchase, valid through August 31."

Always deliver on these promises. An apology without follow-through dents credibility more than no apology at all.

Dealing with Review Bans or Account Suspensions

- **Transparent Communication**
  If Amazon suspends reviews or your account, post a brief

update on your storefront: "We've received unexpected policy notice. We're working urgently with Amazon to restore full service. Thank you for your patience."

- **Structured Appeal**
  Prepare a concise Plan of Action: root-cause analysis, corrective steps, preventive measures. Present it to Amazon support. A well-crafted, humble but confident appeal can shorten downtime and reassure customers once service resumes.

Rebuilding Trust Over Time

- **Highlight Success Stories**
  After resolution, showcase testimonials from customers who appreciated your responsiveness. A mini-case study in your A+ Content—"How we turned a shipping glitch into a faster delivery promise"—demonstrates growth.

- **Solicit Post-Fix Feedback**
  Reach out to buyers affected by the issue, ask for updated ratings after the fix. Many will upgrade their reviews in recognition of your care.

An apology, when performed with genuine care and decisive action, transforms potential reputational ruin into a demonstration of your brand's commitment to customers.

Conclusion: The Prince of Perception

Machiavelli declared that **appearance** often outweighs reality. On Amazon, this counsel is paramount. Behind the scenes, you may be wielding every Machiavellian weapon—stealth tactics, pricing gambits, algorithm exploits—but on the listing, storefront and in every buyer interaction, you must radiate integrity, competence and care.

By meticulously crafting your brand's public face, polishing every customer touchpoint, enlisting credible partners in influencers and press, and mastering the art of the sincere apology, you build an unassailable illusion of virtue. That illusion is your greatest asset—a shield that deflects scrutiny and fosters loyalty, allowing your ruthless strategies to operate undetected beneath the veneer of trustworthiness.

Remember Machiavelli's final word on image: "It is unnecessary for a prince to have all the good qualities I have enumerated, but it is very necessary to appear to have them." Appear virtuous… and your empire on Amazon becomes all but invincible.

Chapter 9: Never Trust the Marketplace

"He who builds his fortress upon the people is never safe."
— Niccolò Machiavelli, *The Prince*

In the world Machiavelli inhabited, allegiances were fleeting, and the only lasting guarantor of power was the ruler's own strategy and strength. Today's Amazon seller faces a similar reality: the marketplace is not a partner, but an ever-shifting Emperor whose favor can vanish overnight. It may reward you with a flood of traffic one day and revoke your Buy Box the next. To rely solely on Amazon—to "build your castle on rented land"—is to court disaster. True security comes from diversification, from controlling your channels, and from knowing when to abandon a lost cause in favor of new opportunities.

This chapter explores four critical lessons:

1. **Amazon Is Not Your Ally — It's the Emperor, Not Your Friend**

2. **Diversify Channels (Shopify, Retail, Wholesale)**

3. **Don't Build Your Castle on Rented Land**

4. **When to Leave a Product Behind and Shift to a New Line or New Model**

1. Amazon Is Not Your Ally — It's the Emperor, Not Your Friend

Machiavelli made clear that princes should never trust those more powerful than themselves. The marketplace, like a monarch, delegates power arbitrarily and can rescind it without warning. When Amazon grants you a prime ranking or Buy Box share, do not mistake that for friendship. It is a temporary privilege, granted to those whose metrics please the algorithm's inscrutable standards.

The Illusion of Stability

- **Algorithmic Whims**
  One week your ads may perform at break-even ACOS; the next, a shift in bidding dynamics or a minor policy change can send your costs skyrocketing.

- **Policy Changes**
  Amazon's TOS evolves constantly. A new regulation on review solicitation, image requirements, or hazardous materials can instantly invalidate your most profitable products.

- **Account Health Risks**
  A handful of negative reviews, a late shipment rate slightly above threshold, or an ill-advised response to a customer message can trigger a warning or suspension. Amazon

does not negotiate; it enforces.

Machiavelli warned that "a wise prince ought to choose those in whom there is least cause of suspicion." But Amazon demands that you place all your trust in its opaque systems—and punishes you the moment you slip. Recognize this: the platform is the Emperor; the moment you forget that, you risk losing everything.

Strategies for Mitigating Dependence

- **Maintain a Cash Reserve**
  Emergencies come without notice: a suspension, a lost vendor relationship, or a global supply chain disruption. Keep funds aside to weather these storms.

- **Develop Direct Relationships**
  Whenever possible, collect customer emails (through compliant insert cards) and foster direct engagement. These buyers can be nurtured outside Amazon if necessary.

- **Monitor Your Account Like Royalty Monitored the Court**
  Track all health metrics daily. Set alerts for any dip in performance or policy changes. Never assume that yesterday's favor carries into tomorrow.

2. Diversify Channels (Shopify, Retail, Wholesale)

To survive when the Emperor overturns his court, you need alternative seats of power. Diversified channels ensure that when Amazon ceases to favor you, your business continues to thrive.

Direct-to-Consumer with Shopify

- **Complete Control Over Brand Experience**
  On your own website, you determine pricing, presentation, promotions, and customer journey. No detail is subject to Amazon's guidelines.

- **Data Ownership**
  Access to granular analytics—visitor behavior, purchase paths, email open rates—allows you to refine marketing in ways Amazon never reveals.

- **Higher Margins**
  Without Amazon's referral and fulfillment fees, your profit per unit can increase significantly, funding further growth across all channels.

Tactical Steps

1. **Set Up a Branded Storefront**
   Use a clean, mobile-optimized theme that mirrors your Amazon aesthetic. Create dedicated landing pages for

your top SKUs.

2. **Bundle & Upsell**
   Offer bundles or subscription plans unavailable on
   Amazon to encourage higher cart values.

3. **Traffic Generation**
   Deploy paid social, Google Ads, or content marketing.
   Leverage SEO by publishing how-to guides, user stories,
   or comparison articles that rank for long-tail keywords.

Wholesale Distribution

- **Access to Brick-and-Mortar Retailers**
  Gym supply stores, specialized boutiques, or big-box
  chains can introduce your brand to audiences who distrust
  online marketplaces.

- **Bulk Order Stability**
  Retailers order in larger quantities, smoothing out the
  peaks and troughs of ecommerce demand.

- **Brand Legitimacy**
  Presence on store shelves enhances consumer
  perception, boosting credibility even on Amazon.

Tactical Steps

1. **Create a Wholesale Catalog**
   Showcase your top products, pricing tiers, and minimum

order quantities. Highlight your brand story and proven Amazon success.

2. **Target Niche Retailers First**
   Pitch independent stores or regional chains that specialize in your category—these are easier to onboard than national giants.

3. **Support Your Partners**
   Provide POS displays, training materials, and marketing assets. The more invested they are in showcasing your products, the more orders you'll receive.

Alternative Marketplaces

- **eBay, Walmart Marketplace, Etsy (for certain products), and Newegg**
  Each platform has its own buyer base and rules. By listing where your product makes sense, you reduce reliance on any single channel.

- **International Expansion**
  Use Amazon's global marketplaces (e.g., Canada, Europe, Japan) or independent local platforms. A suspension in the U.S. markets doesn't have to halt your entire business.

3. Don't Build Your Castle on Rented Land

Machiavelli cautioned against constructing fortresses on terrain controlled by another power—an apt metaphor for over-reliance on any third-party platform. No matter how generous the terms today, that ground can be reclaimed at any moment.

Risks of Rented Land

- **Fee Increases**
  Amazon can raise referral, storage, or program fees with minimal warning, squeezing your margins.

- **Policy Shifts**
  Compliance requirements can change overnight, rendering entire product lines unsellable.

- **Platform Competition**
  Amazon itself sells private label products that directly compete with yours. A new AmazonBasics line can undercut you instantly.

Principles for Reducing Exposure

1. **Own Your Audience**
   The single greatest asset you can build is a tribe of loyal customers. Use email marketing, social media communities, and branded apps to communicate directly.

2. **Invest in Brand Equity**
   A strong brand transcends any one platform. Trademark your logo, invest in PR outreach, and build recognition that drives customers to your site or stores, not just to your Amazon page.

3. **Maintain Operational Independence**
   While Fulfillment by Amazon (FBA) offers convenience, consider a hybrid model that includes merchant fulfillment (FBM). That way, if Amazon suspends FBA, you have an alternative routing for orders.

---

4. When to Leave a Product Behind and Shift to a New Line or New Model

No empire lasts forever, and no product stays profitable for life. Just as a prince must know when to abandon a failing province, an Amazon seller must recognize when to sunset a product before it drains resources and damages brand reputation.

Indicators It's Time to Move On

- **Declining Margins**
  Rising cost of goods sold, combined with shrinking permissible pricing power, warns of a category in decline.

- **Stagnant or Falling Sales Velocity**
  A plateau in unit sales despite increased ad spend signals

market saturation—or commoditization.

- **Rising Returns or Negative Reviews**
  Product fatigue or quality issues can lead to a flood of complaints that tarnish your brand.

- **Regulatory or Compliance Changes**
  New safety rules, labeling requirements, or restrictions may make continued sales uneconomical.

Machiavelli taught that "the wise prince should rely on what he controls, not on the goodwill of others." When your product's fate is tied to factors outside your control—regulations, Amazon policy, consumer taste—it is time to pivot.

Strategies for Exiting Gracefully

1. **Phase Out Inventory**
   Don't abruptly disappear—run promotions, bundle clearance deals, and liquidate remaining stock at acceptable margins.

2. **Leverage Customer Lists**
   Notify your existing buyers of upcoming replacements or upgrades. Offer trade-in discounts or loyalty perks to move them toward your next generation of products.

3. **Harvest Learnings**
   Analyze what worked—features, messaging, channels—and apply those insights to your new launches.

Planting Seeds for the Next Line

- **Continuous Market Research**
  Use product-research tools to identify adjacent niches with growth potential.

- **Pilot Launches**
  Test early with small runs via Walmart Marketplace or direct on Shopify to gauge demand before full Amazon rollout.

- **Brand Extensions**
  If you built trust in one category—say, travel accessories—you can branch into complementary areas like portable chargers or packing cubes, leveraging existing brand equity.

Conclusion: Sovereignty Through Self-Reliance

Machiavelli's enduring lesson is that true power belongs only to those who build and defend it personally. Amazon can be a lucrative platform, but it is not your realm—it is a rented court. To become a sovereign in your own right, you must diversify channels, own your audience, and know when to abandon creaky product lines. Only then will you achieve the stability and growth that outlives any algorithm or policy shift.

Rule your own empire. Trust yourself, not the marketplace.

Chapter 10: Institutions = Systems

"…a wise prince ought to establish laws and arms, for without these he cannot—and indeed ought not to—possess any state."
— Niccolò Machiavelli, *The Prince*

Machiavelli taught that a ruler's true power lies not in momentary victories but in the institutions he builds to make that power durable. A sudden conquest can be lost through chaos; only systems—laws, processes, loyal agents—can transform a fleeting triumph into a stable reign. For the Amazon seller, the equivalent of Machiavelli's "laws and arms" are **Standard Operating Procedures (SOPs), automation tools, and team workflows**—the backbone of a business that must scale, adapt, and survive assaults from competitors, policy shifts, and marketplace upheavals.

In this chapter, we'll explore:

1. **Why Institutions Matter: Machiavelli on Lasting Authority**

2. **Building SOPs: The Blueprint of Consistency**

3. **Automation: Harnessing Technology as Your Loyal Lieutenant**

4. **Team Workflows: Training Your Court for Efficiency and Loyalty**

---

1. Why Institutions Matter: Machiavelli on Lasting Authority

Machiavelli observed that new princes who rely solely on personal talent and ad hoc alliances rarely maintain power. Without strong institutions, every success requires the ruler's constant presence; every crisis demands reinventing the response. Conversely, durable institutions handle routine operations and guard against unexpected shocks, freeing the prince to focus on strategy.

He wrote, "Finally, those newly acquired dominions which are accustomed to living under a prince's forefathers should be so ordered as to extinguish entirely the memory of the old government and to introduce new methods." In business terms, that means **replacing ad hoc tactics with repeatable systems**. You don't want every decision to hinge on your availability or your mood. You want your brand to operate like clockwork—because well-oiled machines resist disruption.

For an Amazon business, institutions translate into documented, tested, and optimized processes that live outside any one person's head. They ensure that:

- Products are researched objectively, not on a whim.

- Launches follow a predictable sequence that maximizes impact.

- Reviews are solicited and managed in compliance with ever-changing rules.

- Customer issues are resolved swiftly, consistently, and in brand-aligned fashion.

Without these systems, you're building a kingdom on sand: every personnel change, software glitch, or policy update becomes an existential threat.

---

2. Building SOPs: The Blueprint of Consistency

Standard Operating Procedures are the written manuals of your empire. They codify best practices, define every step in a process, and provide a framework for training new team members. Machiavelli emphasized that laws create stability: for the Amazon seller, SOPs are your internal "laws."

Crafting Effective SOPs

1. **Identify Core Processes**
   Begin with the highest-impact functions: product research, supplier onboarding, listing creation, PPC campaign setup, inventory forecasting, customer service triage, and review

solicitation.

2. **Map Each Step in Detail**
   For product research, list every action: logging into Helium10, selecting search filters, analyzing keyword difficulty, calculating margins, comparing supplier quotes, and making a go/no-go decision.

3. **Define Roles and Responsibilities**
   Assign each task to a role—Product Analyst, Listing Specialist, PPC Manager, Customer Care Agent. Clarity in ownership prevents tasks from falling through the cracks.

4. **Include Decision Criteria**
   Embed rules of thumb: "If projected ROI < 30% after PPC costs, reject product." "If CPC > $1.50 for top keywords, pause campaign."

5. **Use Visual Aids Where Helpful**
   Flowcharts, checklists, and screenshots can accelerate training and reduce errors. Machiavelli would appreciate a well-illustrated decree.

6. **Iterate and Improve**
   Treat SOPs as living documents. After each product launch or major campaign, solicit feedback from the team: which steps added value? Which created friction? Update the SOP accordingly.

Benefits of SOPs

- **Scalability**: New hires can ramp up faster, increasing throughput without sacrificing quality.

- **Resilience**: If a key team member departs, the SOP ensures continuity.

- **Compliance**: Documented steps help demonstrate policy adherence to Amazon and reduce the risk of suspensions.

- **Continuous Improvement**: With clear baselines, you can measure process improvements and quantify gains.

Machiavelli wrote that "nothing... is more deservedly praised in a prince than the stability and consistency of his course." In your Amazon empire, SOPs are the bedrock of that consistency.

---

3. Automation: Harnessing Technology as Your Loyal Lieutenant

Even the wisest prince cannot be everywhere at once. Machiavelli recognized that prudent delegation is essential. Today's counterpart is **automation**—software that executes routine tasks 24/7, without error or fatigue.

Key Areas for Automation

1. **Inventory Management**
   Tools like RestockPro or Sellerboard can forecast stock

depletion based on sales velocity, trigger reorder alerts, and even generate purchase orders to suppliers.

2. **Price and Buy Box Monitoring**
   Automated repricers adjust your prices in real time to defend the Buy Box or maintain desired margin thresholds.

3. **Review and Feedback Requests**
   Compliant messaging tools send staggered review requests to buyers who've received their orders, increasing review velocity without manual effort.

4. **Advertising Campaign Management**
   AI-driven PPC platforms optimize bids, pause non-performers, identify negative keywords, and allocate budget toward high-ROI campaigns.

5. **Customer Service Triage**
   Chatbots and helpdesk rules categorize and escalate inquiries, ensuring common issues—tracking requests, return processing—are handled instantly, while complex problems go to human agents.

Implementing Automation Wisely

- **Start Small**: Automate a single process end-to-end before layering on additional tools to avoid complexity overload.

- **Maintain Oversight**: Set guardrails—daily reports that flag anomalies, such as repricer price dips below acceptable minimums.

- **Review Effectiveness**: Regularly audit automated outcomes: Are reorder quantities accurate? Are repricer rules capturing the right thresholds?

Machiavelli extolled those who combine "arms and laws"—today's "arms" are automation tools, your "laws" are the SOPs that configure them. Together, they unleash productivity on a scale no manual process can match.

---

4. Team Workflows: Training Your Court for Efficiency and Loyalty

A prince's stability depends on the loyalty and competence of his courtiers. For an Amazon business, your courtiers are your VAs, contractors, and employees. Lampoon Machiavelli's counsel: choose wisely, train thoroughly, and reward loyalty.

Recruiting Your Team

- **Skill and Culture Fit**: Look beyond technical ability. A VA with e-commerce experience but a "task rather than ownership" mindset may underperform compared to a highly driven newcomer.

- **Clear Expectations**: During hiring, share your SOPs overview and your core values—speed, precision, accountability—so candidates know what success looks like.

Onboarding and Training

1. **Structured Onboarding Plan**
   Week 1: System access, brand overview, key SOP introduction.
   Week 2: Shadow experienced team members on tasks.
   Week 3: Independent execution with mentor feedback.

2. **Mentorship and Pairing**
   Pair new hires with senior team members for bi-weekly check-ins, problem-solving sessions, and career guidance.

3. **Knowledge Repository**
   Maintain a centralized wiki or cloud drive with SOPs, video tutorials, FAQs, and policy updates. Encourage contributions—crowdsourced insights often surface improvements.

Building Loyalty and Clarity

- **Ownership and Autonomy**
  Allow your top performers to propose process enhancements. When VAs see their ideas implemented, their loyalty and engagement skyrocket.

- **Transparent Metrics**
  Share dashboard access showing KPIs tied to each

role—order accuracy rates, ad ROAS, response times—so team members understand how they contribute to the broader mission.

- **Incentives and Recognition**
  Tie bonuses or performance perks to achieving process milestones: perfect QA audits, error-free months, under-budget advertising spend. Recognize individual contributions publicly in team meetings.

Machiavelli noted that princes who "do not provide for insufficient or faulty forces" suffer defeats. Your team workflows ensure that everyone operates at peak effectiveness, leaving no weak links in your supply chain or customer experience.

---

5. Systematizing Key Processes: Research, Launch, and Review Cycles

Institutions shine brightest when they structure the most critical, repetitive cycles of your business. Three cycles demand rigorous systematization:

A. Product Research Cycle

1. **Market Scanning**
   Every quarter, run automated scans for emerging niches—using Helium10 Trendster or Google Trends

APIs—to produce a ranked list of potential categories.

2. **Financial Modeling**
   Apply a standardized spreadsheet template: input landed cost, Amazon fees, ad spend estimates, and target margin. Automatically compute viability scores.

3. **Supplier Sourcing**
   Maintain an approved vendor list with pre-negotiated terms. Trigger RFQs via email templates and compare quotes using a consistent rubric: price, lead time, QC processes.

4. **Test Ordering**
   Execute trial orders under SOP guidelines: quantity, QC sample inspection checklist, lab testing as needed. Deliver a test report before greenlighting bulk orders.

This cycle ensures you pursue only the highest-potential products, cutting off random whims and protecting precious capital.

B. Launch Cycle

1. **Pre-Launch Checklist**

   - Completed listing draft, SEO-optimized title and bullets

   - High-resolution images and A+ Content loaded

- Back-end keywords approved

    - PPC campaigns drafted with agreed budgets and targets

    - Review request flow configured

2. **Launch Execution (Day 0–7)**

    - Activate promotions (coupons, lightning deals) on Day 0

    - Ramp PPC to target ACOS by Day 2

    - Monitor inventory burn rate, adjusting ad spend to maintain steady velocity

3. **Post-Launch Optimization (Day 8–30)**

    - Analyze Search Term Reports, prune non-converting keywords

    - A/B test headline images or bullet order weekly

    - Solicit initial batch of reviews via email follow-up at Day 10

4. **Scaling Phase (Day 31+)**

    - Expand PPC to new match types and channels (DSP, Sponsored Brands)

- o Introduce variation SKUs or bundles

- o Explore external traffic sources informed by early Amazon data

A launch without a system is a guess. A launch with a system is a predictable generator of momentum.

C. Review Management Cycle

1. **Review Solicitation**

   - o Hour 24 post-delivery: send a "thank you" email with care tips (no direct review ask)

   - o Day 10 post-delivery: send a compliant review request, timed by purchase date

2. **Review Monitoring**

   - o Automated daily digest of new reviews

   - o Tag negative reviews for immediate follow-up

3. **Exception Handling**

   - o For any 1–3 star review: open a support ticket, offer replacement or refund

- Log root cause in a central database (shipping damage, product defect, misunderstanding)

4. **Feedback Loop**

   - Weekly review of review data: identify trends in complaints

   - Interface with product development or QC to implement design changes

   - Publicly update A+ Content to reflect improvements

Reviews are not passive; they are signals to the algorithm and feedback from customers. A systemized cycle turns raw sentiment into actionable intelligence and sustained ranking.

Conclusion: From Ad Hoc to Unstoppable

Machiavelli's enduring wisdom is that power lies in institutions, not personalities. For the Amazon seller, institutions manifest as SOPs, automation, disciplined team workflows, and rigorously systematized cycles of research, launch, and review. These systems transform scattered effort into unbreakable processes—processes that survive personnel changes, navigate policy storms, and outpace competitors.

Implement these institutions with the resolve of a prince codifying his laws. Document every step. Delegate with clarity. Automate without losing oversight. Continuously refine. In doing so, you build an Amazon empire not dependent on chance or heroics, but empowered by structure—an empire that endures long after individual battles are won or lost.

Chapter 11: Guard Against Revolt (Bad Reviews & Crises)

"The people must be kept friendly, for one has no secure way to hold them otherwise."
— Niccolò Machiavelli, *The Prince*

No ruler can rely solely on conquest to maintain control. In Machiavelli's world, as soon as a prince neglects the loyalty of his subjects, plots form, revolts ignite, and everything he's built can collapse overnight. The Amazon marketplace is no different. Your customers—your "subjects"—are fickle, empowered to broadcast complaints to thousands, and quick to abandon brands that disappoint. A sudden surge of bad reviews, a single viral complaint, or an unresolved crisis can topple your best-performing listing in days.

This chapter unpacks how to proactively guard against customer revolt, respond swiftly to critical feedback, and wield Amazon's own tools—Vine, product updates, refunds—as political levers to preserve order. We'll explore:

1. **Understanding the Speed and Scale of Revolt**

2. **Rapid Response to Critical Reviews and Negative Seller Feedback**

3. **Vine and Early Reviewer Programs as Stabilizers**

4. **Product Updates and Iterations to Demonstrate Commitment**

5. **Refunds and Replacements as Instruments of Reassurance**

---

1. Understanding the Speed and Scale of Revolt

Machiavelli observed that "the masses are always taken by appearances, and the outcome of actions, more than by the realities." On Amazon, appearance is everything: star ratings, review counts, product ranking, and social buzz form the visible tapestry customers use to judge you. Meanwhile, the true state of your product—its quality, your backend acumen—remains hidden.

A single 1-star review can trigger a cascade:

- **Algorithmic Impact**: A cluster of negative reviews depresses your average rating. Amazon's algorithm downgrades your Buy Box eligibility and organic ranking.

- **Social Signaling**: Potential buyers see low ratings and avoid your listing, leading to reduced sales velocity and further ranking penalties.

- **Competitive Opportunity**: Rivals pounce, boosting ad spend to seize traffic you abandon, capturing dissatisfied buyers looking for alternatives.

Revolt spreads at digital speed—no court intrigue, no slow mobilization. A mid-afternoon complaint can erupt into a trending thread by evening. Recognizing this urgency, you must build defenses that operate in real time.

---

2. Rapid Response to Critical Reviews and Negative Seller Feedback

Machiavelli taught that the signs of discontent must be snuffed out early. A prince who ignores rumors of rebellion finds himself surrounded by conspirators. Similarly, the Amazon seller must treat every critical review and negative seller feedback as an insurrectionary spark.

A. Monitoring and Triage

- **Automated Alerts**: Configure tools to notify you within minutes of any new 1- or 2-star review, or any new negative seller feedback. Real-time SMS or email alerts ensure no crisis goes unnoticed.

- **Categorize by Severity**: Not all bad reviews carry equal weight. If a review highlights a shipping delay, urgency differs from one describing a fundamental product defect. Tag each incident accordingly—Logistics, Quality, Misleading Listing, etc.

B. The Four-Step Crisis Response

1. **Acknowledge**
   Publicly acknowledge the reviewer's experience by responding on the review itself if Amazon permits, or via a comment on the listing. Use their name, validate their feelings, and promise to investigate:
   "Hi Sarah, I'm sorry to hear about your experience with our camping stove. Thank you for bringing this to our attention—your safety is our top priority."

2. **Empathize and Apologize**
   A genuine apology defuses anger. Machiavelli noted that "a prince cannot always appear generous, but must always seem to be so." In practice:
   "I understand how frustrating it is to receive a product that doesn't work as promised. Please accept our sincere apologies."

3. **Offer Resolution**
   Present a clear path to resolution: replacement, refund, or technical support. If it's a product defect:
   "We'd like to send you a replacement stove free of charge. Alternatively, if you prefer a refund, we can process it immediately—no questions asked."

4. **Follow Through and Follow Up**
   Execute the resolution without delay. Once the replacement ships or refund processes, follow up:
   "Your replacement order has shipped with expedited delivery. Please let me know when you receive it—or if you have any further concerns."

Encourage the customer to update their review if satisfied. Many will revise a 1-star to 3–4 stars simply because they feel heard and cared for.

By employing this rapid-response framework, you demonstrate to both the aggrieved customer and onlooking buyers that you command the realm with competence and compassion.

---

3. Vine and Early Reviewer Programs as Stabilizers

Just as Machiavelli advised princes to secure the loyalty of key citizens, Amazon sellers can enlist structured programs to shore up their reputations—namely, Amazon Vine and the Early Reviewer Program.

A. Amazon Vine: The Trusted Council

- **Selective Enrollment**
  Only enroll your hero SKUs—those with proven demand and stable supply. Vine reviewers are handpicked and often more critical; use Vine to build a solid base of honest, high-quality reviews before open launch.

- **Early Warning Insight**
  Negative Vine reviews are gifts. They highlight genuine flaws before your broader audience sees them. If a Vine reviewer flags a design defect, you can correct it in time to

prevent a flood of public complaints.

B. Early Reviewer Program: The Voices of Reason

- **Sustained Momentum**
  The Early Reviewer Program drives a small stream of
  reviews over time, smoothing out velocity and anchoring
  your average rating above category threshold. Buyers see
  a consistent flow of feedback, signaling stability rather than
  sudden bursts or droughts.

These programs function like Machiavelli's elite guards—trusted
advisors whose insights and endorsements strengthen your hold
on the marketplace.

---

4. Product Updates and Iterations to Demonstrate Commitment

A wise ruler never ignores defects in the realm's infrastructure.
Machiavelli urged that "men change their rulers in hope of better
fortune." If your product remains flawed, buyers will defect to
competitors promising a superior experience.

A. Centralized Feedback Logging

- **Issue Database**
  Log every complaint—Vine, Early Reviewer, organic
  reviews, and customer service tickets—into a central

system. Tag issues by category: Design, Packaging, Instructions, Shipping.

- **Trend Analysis**
  Weekly, analyze the volume and severity of each complaint type. Prioritize top three issues this quarter.

B. Agile Iteration Process

1. **Root-Cause Investigation**
   For each priority issue, dissect the supply chain and design specs. If stoves leak fuel, is the seal flawed or the shipping orientation to blame?

2. **Prototype and Test**
   Engage your supplier to produce revised samples. Conduct in-house stress tests or third-party lab assessments.

3. **Small-Batch Pilot**
   Ship updated units to a control group—either internal testers or a subset of loyal customers—and collect feedback before full-scale rollout.

4. **Version Release and Announcement**
   When you launch the improved model, update your listing prominently:
   "Now featuring our upgraded leak-proof seal, based on customer feedback!"
   This transparency shows customers you listen and act.

By iterating visibly and communicating openly, you preempt revolts—customers see continuous improvement rather than stagnation.

---

5. Refunds and Replacements as Instruments of Reassurance

Machiavelli recognized that a forgiving ruler can convert hostility into loyalty. In Amazon's realm, **refunds and replacements** are your acts of clemency. Handled strategically, they restore faith and keep your ratings intact.

A. The Refund/Replacements Policy Framework

- **No-Questions-Asked Windows**
  Offer a 30- or 60-day refund window—clear, generous, and prominently displayed in your policy. Buyers gain confidence: they know they have an escape hatch if things go awry.

- **Accelerated Processing**
  Automate refund approvals for orders under a certain value or with specified issue codes. Avoid manual red tape that frustrates customers.

B. Diplomatic Communication

- **Preemptive Outreach**
  If you detect a shipment delay or product batch issue, email affected customers with an apology and offer a partial refund or expedited replacement before they complain. This proactive approach often stops negative reviews before they form.

- **Follow-Up Feedback**
  After a replacement arrives, request confirmation of satisfaction. A brief note—*"Happy to see you received the new unit! Please let me know if it meets your expectations."*—reinforces goodwill.

C. Calculated Generosity

- **Cost-Benefit Analysis**
  While refunds and replacements incur costs, the lifetime value of a retained customer—and the avoided damage of a public 1-star review—often exceeds that expense.

- **Abuse Mitigation**
  To prevent exploitation, track serial returners or replacement requests. For repeat offenders without genuine issues, offer troubleshooting steps first and reserve full refunds for verifiable defects.

By wielding refunds and replacements with both generosity and discernment, you convert potential rebellions into opportunities for allegiance.

Conclusion: Maintaining the Throne Through Vigilance and Responsiveness

In *The Prince*, Machiavelli warned that "the prince who relies entirely on good faith breaks down as soon as others deceive him." Today's Amazon seller must recognize that customers and the algorithm will test the limits of their goodwill constantly. Revolt—manifested as bad reviews, negative feedback, and rank declines—can erupt without warning. Only through vigilant monitoring, rapid and empathetic response, strategic use of Amazon's stabilizing programs, visible product improvement, and judicious acts of refund or replacement can you keep your subjects content and your empire secure.

Your kingdom is not the products you sell, but the trust you earn. Guard against revolt by demonstrating, every day, that you see, listen, and act. In doing so, you will not merely react to crises—you will transform them into proof of your enduring commitment, solidifying your reign in the hearts and carts of your customers.

Chapter 12: Adapt or Die

"A prince who is not wise himself cannot be wisely advised."
— Niccolò Machiavelli, *The Prince*

In *The Prince*, Machiavelli warns that wisdom is the foundation of all enduring power. Without it, even the shrewdest counsel falls flat, and the ruler is driven by fickle advisors into ruinous mistakes. On Amazon, this lesson could not be more urgent: the only constant is change. Policies shift without notice, algorithms mutate, new tools appear, and consumer preferences pivot on a dime. If you, the Amazon seller, do not cultivate your own wisdom—by staying vigilant, mastering data, and making ruthless decisions—you will be outpaced, outmaneuvered, and eventually extinguished by those who adapt more swiftly.

This chapter arms you with the mindset and the processes to evolve continually. We'll explore:

1. **The Wise Prince: Owning Your Expertise**

2. **Staying Ahead of Amazon's Shifting Rules**

3. **Decoding Algorithmic Currents**

4. **Embracing New Tools as Strategic Weapons**

5. **Data-Driven Ruthlessness: How to Make and Execute Hard Calls**

6. **Pruning the Herd: Killing Underperforming SKUs**

7. **Embedding Adaptability into Your Organization**

---

1. The Wise Prince: Owning Your Expertise

Machiavelli asserts that a prince must be the fount of wisdom himself. If he relies entirely on ministers or advisors, he is vulnerable to deceit or negligence. Translated to ecommerce, this means you cannot outsource all strategic thinking to consultants, software, or VAs—you must internalize the levers that drive success on Amazon. This begins with:

- **Personal Mastery of Core Metrics**
  Understand ACOS, TACoS, conversion rates, click-through percentages, review velocity, Buy Box share. Don't glance at dashboards; drill into their mechanics until you can predict how a 1% shift in PPC bids will affect your margin or ranking.

- **Regular Self-Education**
  Set aside weekly "war-room" sessions to read policy updates, attend webinars from Amazon or third-party experts, and dissect case studies of sellers who have navigated recent upheavals.

- **Cultivating Strategic Judgment**
  Wisdom, Machiavelli notes, is not mere knowledge but the ability to discern which counsel to follow. Train yourself to spot consensus traps—"everyone says Sponsored Display is the future"—and instead test, measure, and decide based on your own data.

By becoming your own oracle, you reduce the lag between insight and action. In Machiavelli's terms, you cease being a passive vessel and become an active architect of your fate.

---

2. Staying Ahead of Amazon's Shifting Rules

Amazon's Terms of Service and program policies are dynamic, often changing without a formal announcement. Ignorance is no excuse—violations can lead to suppressed listings, account suspensions, or outright bans. To prevent policy pitfalls:

A. Establish a Policy-Watch Regiment

- **Daily Policy Digest**
  Assign a team member to scan Amazon's Seller Central bulletins, the "News & Updates" widget, and specialized forums. Summarize any changes and circulate an internal memo each morning.

- **Monthly Compliance Audits**
  Map each active tactic—review solicitation, PPC
  strategies, image formats—against the latest policy
  language. If a method is flagged as "under review" or
  "deprecated," begin phasing it out immediately.

B. Anticipating Hidden Shifts

- **Shadow Compliance Testing**
  Periodically run controlled experiments: send a batch of
  review requests with slightly different wording to see if
  Amazon's automated filter flags them; upload a test image
  with minor text overlay to confirm that the style guide still
  prohibits it.

- **Legal and Tax Watch**
  Beyond Amazon's own rules, new import tariffs, product
  safety regulations, or privacy laws (e.g., GDPR-like
  measures in new markets) can hobble your operations.
  Subscribe to regulatory newsletters in each country you
  sell into and integrate a compliance calendar into your
  SOPs.

Machiavelli would see this as fortifying your castle walls before the
siege begins. You cannot wait for a policy ambush to force you
onto the defensive.

3. Decoding Algorithmic Currents

The Amazon algorithm is a living beast: it prioritizes relevance, performance, and customer satisfaction metrics in a constantly shifting mix. You cannot treat it as a static formula; you must learn to read its mood swings and surf its waves.

A. Tracking Ranking Signals

- **Weekly Keyword Rank Reports**
  Generate automated snapshots of your ASIN's position for each high-value keyword. Plot trends over time. A sudden drop in ranking for a core term is a red flag—often indicating new competition, a price issue, or a backend listing error.

- **Buy Box Win Rate Monitoring**
  Chart your Buy Box percentage hourly. If the rate dips below your threshold, correlate the timing against repricer logs, inventory levels, and recent feedback to pinpoint the cause.

B. Experimentation and Feedback Loops

- **A/B Title and Image Tests**
  Use Amazon's Manage Your Experiments tool or a third-party solution to run title or image variations simultaneously. Evaluate not just sales lift but also click-through rate and time-on-page metrics to sense shifts

in visitor engagement.

- **Promotion and Coupon Analysis**
  Schedule regular pulses of coupons, lightning deals, or Prime Exclusive discounts. Measure the lift in sales velocity and review generation, then regress the data to optimize future timing, depth of discount, and targeting.

By treating the algorithm as an adaptive adversary rather than a set-and-forget mechanism, you stay in tune with its preferences, maintaining momentum where others stall.

---

4. Embracing New Tools as Strategic Weapons

Every year, dozens of new software platforms and services launch to serve Amazon sellers. Some are vaporware; some become indispensable. Machiavelli extols the prince who equips himself with the best arms—today's arms are analytics, automation, and intelligence tools.

A. Evaluating Tool ROI

- **Pilot Periods with Metrics Gates**
  Trial each new platform for 30 days, applying it to a controlled subset of SKUs. Predefine success criteria—15% reduction in ACoS, 20% boost in keyword coverage, 50% faster response to customer

messages—and only integrate tools that meet those
benchmarks.

- **Integration into SOPs**
  Once a tool is approved, update your SOPs to include it.
  For example, if you adopt a new repricer, specify the exact
  rules, escalation paths, and audit intervals to prevent
  runaway price wars.

B. Continuous Scouting and Vetting

- **Vendor Conferences and Beta Programs**
  Attend industry events and join private beta programs to
  see emerging tools before the general market. Early
  access grants tactical advantage—like exploring new
  territory before rivals arrive.

- **Cross-Team Knowledge Sharing**
  Weekly "tech demos" within your team allow members
  who discover useful features to teach others, accelerating
  adoption and generating new use cases.

In Machiavelli's parlance, attract the best mercenary captains,
then ensure they swear loyalty to your cause. The right tools,
wielded under your command, become force multipliers that keep
you steps ahead of competitors.

5. Data-Driven Ruthlessness: How to Make and Execute Hard Calls

Wisdom without execution is empty talk. Once you've armed yourself with data—from Helium10 search volumes to Jungle Scout competitor intelligence—you must be prepared to act swiftly and decisively.

A. Establishing Clear Performance Thresholds

- **Minimum Viable Metrics**
  Define the barest acceptable performance: a 3% conversion rate, 1.2% profit margin after all fees, 80% Buy Box win rate at or below target ACOS. These thresholds become your line in the sand.

- **Automated Alerts and Escalations**
  Configure dashboards to trigger immediate alerts whenever a metric crosses below your threshold. The alert routes to specific team members responsible for mitigation—PPC lead, listing specialist, customer care agent—each empowered to act without delay.

B. Decisive Execution

1. **Pause or Cancel Underperforming Campaigns**
   If a Sponsored Products campaign exceeds your ACOS threshold for three consecutive days, pause it. Don't wait for a weekly review—cut losses as soon as the data

demands it.

2. **Reprice or Suspend Wobbly Listings**
   A listing whose organic sessions drop by more than 20%
   week over week signals shifting traffic patterns.
   Immediately analyze the listing for errors, competitor
   moves, or ad budget reallocation—and take corrective
   action within 24 hours.

3. **Swift Supply Chain Adjustments**
   If landed costs rise due to freight surcharges, re-negotiate
   with alternate providers, increase unit pricing, or shift
   production to a different facility. Do not endure margin
   erosion while you seek approval from higher-ups.

Machiavelli would applaud such uncompromising vigor: "Tardiness often robs us opportunity," he wrote. Your decisions must match that urgency—proactive, data-steeped, and unflinchingly carried out.

---

6. Pruning the Herd: Killing Underperforming SKUs

Just as a prince must excise decadent provinces to prevent the rot from spreading, you must ruthlessly remove products that drain resources and drag down aggregate metrics.

A. Identifying Candidates for Sunset

- **SKU Profitability Audits**
  Quarterly, run a P&L drill-down by SKU. Identify any with negative net profit after all costs—including advertising, storage fees, returns, and overhead.

- **Stagnant Momentum Checks**
  Highlight SKUs whose 90-day rolling average of units sold is below 20% of their peak month. Products that cannot sustain baseline traction are anchors, not engines.

B. Exit Strategies

1. **Order Liquidation with Margin Floor**
   Bundle residual stock with accessories or partner products at a controlled discount, ensuring you recuperate at least your landed cost. Avoid fire-sale pricing that trains buyers to wait for rock-bottom deals.

2. **Use External Channels**
   Funnel slow-moving inventory to outlets like eBay, Walmart Marketplace, or B2B wholesale partners. This preserves Amazon metrics while clearing your shelves.

3. **Archive Listings on Amazon**
   Once stock is liquidated, fully remove the ASIN from active status. Leaving a dormant listing invites hijackers, outdated reviews, and policy flags.

C. Redeploying Capital

- **Reinvest in Winners**
  Redirect the freed budget toward high-velocity SKUs—boost ad spend where ACOS remains healthy, increase inventory orders to avoid stockouts, and explore expansion into complementary variations.

- **Fund New Tests**
  Allocate a portion of the capital saved from pruning to seed-quantity launches of new products, maintaining the cycle of innovation and growth.

Machiavelli urged that "he who becomes a prince through the favor of the populace must keep them friendly," but those who cling to every asset without discrimination invite decay. Prune boldly to keep your catalogue strong and focused.

---

7. Embedding Adaptability into Your Organization

Lasting adaptability is not an individual quirk but a cultural muscle. You must weave flexibility into the very DNA of your team and processes.

A. Institutionalizing Continuous Improvement

- **Monthly "After-Action Reviews"**
  Hold structured sessions after every major launch, policy change, or crisis. Document what succeeded, what failed, and what you will do differently next time. Feed those lessons back into your SOPs within 48 hours.

- **Cross-Functional Task Forces**
  When a new Amazon program or tool emerges, assemble a rapid-response team—PPC, listing, inventory, legal—to evaluate, pilot, and either adopt or dismiss the innovation within a set timeframe.

B. Incentivizing Adaptation

- **Performance Bonuses for Learning Milestones**
  Reward team members who complete certifications (Amazon DSP, Advertising Console), publish insightful analytics reports, or lead successful beta tests of new tools.

- **Rotation Programs**
  Rotate high-potential employees through different roles—customer service, marketing, operations—to build a holistic understanding of the business. This prevents siloed thinking and sparks cross-pollination of ideas.

C. Leadership by Example

Machiavelli praised princes who "throw themselves into the thick of the fight." As the head of your Amazon enterprise, you must lead adaptation efforts personally: champion new tool adoption, participate in policy review meetings, and be the first to execute on hard decisions. Your example signals to the team that adaptability is not optional but the highest duty.

Conclusion: Thrive by Evolving

In the ruthless marketplace of Amazon, the moment you stand still, you begin to fall behind. Machiavelli's admonition—that a prince needs his own wisdom to survive—rings truer than ever. By mastering policy shifts, decoding algorithmic signals, harnessing the latest tools, making data-driven decisions, and pruning your product line without mercy, you cultivate an organization that does more than react to change—it anticipates and shapes it. Embed adaptability into your culture, and you transform every threat into opportunity. Fail to do so, and the tide of competition, policy, and technology will sweep you away.

Adapt or die: the marketplace demands nothing less.

Chapter 13: The Machiavellian Exit Plan

"Men judge more by the eye than by the hand, because everyone can see, but few can feel… And everybody sees what you appear to be, but few experience what you really are."
— Niccolò Machiavelli, *The Prince*

Even in Machiavelli's era, exit strategies weighed heavily on the minds of ambitious rulers. Some secured their legacy by passing power gracefully; others grasped at their thrones until the bitter end. For the Amazon seller, a successful exit—knowing when to sell, how to maximize value, and how to depart on one's own terms—requires the same ruthless calculation that built the empire in the first place. Growing a brand purely for vanity is folly; true strength lies in recognizing the moment when further expansion delivers diminishing returns and unlocks greater value through a strategic sale.

This chapter guides you through the three pillars of a Machiavellian exit:

1. **Knowing When to Sell**

2. **Positioning Your Brand for Acquisition**

3. **Cleaning Up the Books, Building Defensibility, Packaging Your Narrative**

1. Knowing When to Sell: Don't Grow for Vanity

Machiavelli counseled princes to avoid ambition that outstrips their means. "It is an argument of great folly to expect safety in repose from the very men whose safety you have taken away," he warned—meaning that unchecked conquest sows insecurity. On Amazon, growth for its own sake can be intoxicating: new SKUs, new markets, new programs. But each expansion brings complexity, risk, and capital tied up in inventory. A seller who stretches too thin can expose the business to supply chain disruptions, margin erosion, and managerial overwhelm.

Signs You've Reached the Apex

- **Plateauing Cash-on-Cash Returns**
  If each additional advertising dollar or product line yields lower incremental profit than your cost of capital, you've entered the zone of diminishing returns. Growth beyond this point creates vanity metrics—revenue growth without corresponding bottom-line expansion.

- **Complexity Overload**
  When product portfolios exceed your operational bandwidth, error rates climb. Late shipments, mispriced listings, and delayed responses become chronic. Machiavelli noted that a prince who expands his territories too widely without sufficient administration invites revolt

and decay.

- **Market Saturation and Competitive Encroachment**
  If your category sees a flood of entrants and margin
  compression, the effort required to defend each SKU may
  outstrip the benefits. The battle for incremental market
  share becomes a war of attrition better ended in profit
  realization.

The Wisdom of Strategic Withdrawal

Machiavelli wrote, "Men in general judge more by the eye than by
the hand." What matters in an exit is not simply the numbers but
the narrative—in the eyes of acquirers, a brand that exhibits
disciplined, profitable growth is far more attractive than one that
chases every new trend. Recognizing when you have built a
valuable, defensible position—and resisting the urge to
overextend—is the mark of a wise entrepreneur.

---

2. Positioning Your Brand for Acquisition

Once you've concluded that selling represents the highest-return
path, you must position your brand as a prize no buyer can refuse.
Machiavelli admired princes who prepared their domains for
smooth succession; you too must prepare your Amazon business
for seamless transfer to FBA aggregators, private equity groups,
or direct-to-consumer (DTC) players.

Understanding Potential Buyers

- **FBA Aggregators**
  These roll-up specialists value stable cash flows, strong brand equity, and scalable operations. They pay multiples of Seller SDE (seller discretionary earnings) and prize businesses with proven Amazon performance, high degree of automation, and defensible listing positions.

- **Private Equity (PE)**
  PE firms look for businesses with clear expansion levers beyond Amazon—such as retail distribution, international growth, or proprietary product lines. They demand rigorous financial controls and growth playbooks.

- **Direct-to-Consumer Brands**
  Larger DTC players may acquire complementary Amazon-first brands to fill portfolio gaps, add new customer segments, or leverage cross-selling. They assess brand loyalty, social media following, and owned-traffic potential.

Crafting a Buyer-Centric Value Proposition

Machiavelli counseled that a prince must appear as capable as he seems; to buyers, your numbers must tell a coherent, compelling story:

1. **Consistent, Predictable Cash Flows**
   Demonstrate month-over-month and year-over-year revenue and profit stability. Minimize seasonality spikes or

show a clear strategy to manage them (e.g., product mix that offsets cyclical dips).

2. **Clean, Automated Operations**
   Buyers value businesses that run without the founder's constant intervention. Highlight your SOPs, automated repricers, and staff structure. If you can step away and the business hums along, you command a premium.

3. **Defensible Market Position**
   Show why customers choose your brand: trademark protection, unique formulations or designs, high review ratings, and a loyal repeat-customer base. Demonstrate categories or sub-niches where you hold top-three rank.

4. **Growth Roadmap**
   Provide a clear blueprint for future expansion: untapped geographies, new sales channels, product line extensions, or marketing channels (email, influencer partnerships). Buyers are buying tomorrow's potential as much as today's reality.

By packaging your business as a turnkey asset with runway for growth, you shift from a seller in need of an exit to an owner of a must-have asset.

3. Cleaning Up Your Books, Building Defensibility, Packaging Your Narrative

Machiavelli emphasized the power of perception. Just as a prince presents a polished court to visiting dignitaries, you must present a pristine, well-documented business to potential acquirers.

Financial and Legal Due Diligence

- **Reconcile and Simplify Financials**
  Consolidate revenues and expenses into clear categories: Amazon sales, referral and fulfillment fees, advertising costs, COGS, overhead. Eliminate personal expenses or extraordinary items. Buyers expect clean profit-and-loss statements and balance sheets, preferably prepared or audited by a reputable accountant.

- **Evidence of Compliance**
  Document your compliance with Amazon policies, intellectual property registrations, and any regulatory requirements (e.g., FDA for supplements). Provide a record of past account health warnings and their resolutions, demonstrating proactive governance.

- **Inventory Accounting**
  Detail your inventory valuation method, turnover ratios, and any potential write-down obligations. Buyers will want visibility into aging SKUs and a plan for their disposition.

Strengthening Defensibility

- **Intellectual Property Portfolio**
  Secure trademarks in key markets. If you have proprietary formulas or designs, obtain patents or maintain detailed trade-secret documentation. The stronger your IP position, the higher the entry barrier and the greater your leverage.

- **Supplier and Distributor Agreements**
  Demonstrate long-term contracts with favorable terms. Buyers worry about supplier concentration risk; showing multiple vetted sources reduces their risk premium.

- **Customer Data and Owned Channels**
  Extract and present any audience lists—email subscribers, social media followings, repeat-customer cohorts. The more direct relationships you control, the less buyers fear Amazon policy shifts will decimate your revenue.

Packaging Your Narrative

Machiavelli wrote that "it is not titles that honor men, but men that honor titles." Copy that dynamic by crafting an exit story that transforms your numbers into an inspiring journey:

1. **Founding Myth**
   Concisely narrate your brand's inception—what problem you solved, why you were uniquely qualified, and how you scaled from zero to hero. A compelling origin resonates

with buyers' emotional and strategic motivations.

2. **Key Milestones**
    Highlight major wins: hitting six figures in revenue,
    securing outside funding, winning Amazon's Choice
    badges, launching international expansions, or executing
    innovative marketing campaigns.

3. **Lessons and Legacies**
    Discuss challenges you overcame—supply chain snarls,
    fierce competition, fluctuating ad costs—and how each
    victory strengthened the brand's resilience. This narrative
    shows that the brand can withstand future storms.

4. **Vision for the Future**
    Present a forward-looking three- to five-year roadmap,
    complete with financial projections, required investments,
    and expected ROI. Framing your business as a continuing
    story assures buyers that they're stepping into an ongoing
    opportunity, not a sunset asset.

By combining spotless financials, credible defensibility, and a
riveting narrative, you embody Machiavelli's ideal prince—both
powerful in fact and irresistible in appearance.

Conclusion: Depart on Your Terms

Machiavelli counselled rulers to "act on the spur of the moment"
when opportunity arises, but also to prepare diligently so that

when the moment comes, they are ready. An exit is that pivotal moment for the Amazon seller: the culmination of years of strategy, toil, and daring. Grow not for vanity but for value; position your brand as an asset too attractive to refuse; scrub and document every facet of your business; and weave a narrative that transforms raw data into irresistible opportunity.

When you execute this Machiavellian exit plan—knowing exactly when to sell, how to appeal to the right buyers, and how to present your empire at its most powerful—you ensure that your departure is not an end but a transition to new conquests, with capital and reputation intact to fuel your next venture.

Chapter 14: Teaching Your Successors

"It is not titles that honor men, but men that honor titles."
— Niccolò Machiavelli, *The Prince*

The mark of a truly powerful ruler is not merely the ability to seize and hold power, but to transfer it—seamlessly, securely, and with one's realm intact. Machiavelli emphasized that "the main foundations of all states are good laws and good arms," but a prince who departs without a capable heir risks seeing his achievements unravel in his absence. For the Amazon seller-turned-entrepreneur, the transition from hands-on operator to strategic owner means building a self-sustaining organization capable of thriving without your daily intervention. This chapter lays out how to train your team to run the business, craft the definitive guidebook for your brand—your "Prince's Manual"—and install the managers, processes, and incentives that align everyone's efforts with your long-term vision.

---

1. Training Your Team to Operate Without You

Machiavelli warned that a prince who depends entirely on his personal prowess leaves his state vulnerable the moment he is away or incapacitated. Similarly, if every decision and course of action in your Amazon enterprise flows through you alone, the business cannot survive your departure. To create a resilient organization, you must deliberately cultivate independence in your lieutenants and frontline staff.

Identify Critical Roles and Capabilities

Begin by mapping out the essential functions of your business: product research and sourcing, listing optimization, advertising and promotions, inventory management, customer service, financial oversight, and supply-chain logistics. For each area, identify:

- **Key tasks and decisions**

- **Required skills and knowledge**

- **Dependencies on other functions**

This "capability matrix" shows where single points of failure exist and where training investment is most urgent.

Develop a Structured Training Program

With your critical roles outlined, build a formal training curriculum that blends documented processes with live mentorship:

1. **Core Knowledge Modules**

   - **Amazon Platform Mastery**: Walk through Seller Central navigation, policy updates, account health metrics, and advertising console best practices.

- **Data and Analytics**: Teach your team to read performance dashboards, interpret Helium10 or Jungle Scout reports, and draw actionable insights.

- **Brand Philosophy**: Impart the "why" behind every strategic choice—your values around quality, customer experience, and long-term reputation.

2. **Hands-On Apprenticeship**

- **Shadowing**: New hires spend their first weeks observing you and senior team members handle real tasks—launching a PPC campaign, negotiating with suppliers, responding to a critical review.

- **Guided Execution**: Once they've seen the process, they perform the tasks under supervision, receiving immediate feedback and correction.

3. **Independent Projects**

- Assign each trainee a small-scale initiative—researching a new product idea, redesigning a listing, or managing a limited ad budget. Assess outcomes against predefined metrics and debrief thoroughly.

4. **Regular Check-Ins and Assessments**

- Schedule weekly learning reviews where trainees present what they've learned, challenges faced, and where they need further support. Use these sessions to refine the training content.

By systematizing knowledge transfer, you ensure that every team member internalizes not just the "how," but the "why" behind your methods.

Cultivate Decision-Making Autonomy

Machiavelli extolled the virtue of a prince who "is wise enough to follow good counsel." To equip your team for autonomy:

- **Define Decision Rights**: Create a RACI matrix (Responsible, Accountable, Consulted, Informed) for every process—when can a manager sign off on a new product listing without your approval, and when must they escalate?

- **Scenario Playbooks**: Document how to handle common crises—Buy Box loss, inventory stockout, sudden policy warning—so that team members can act decisively without having to "ask the boss."

- **Post-Mortem Culture**: After each major decision or campaign, hold a blameless review. Encourage staff to analyze results, share learnings, and adapt processes, reinforcing that smart risk-taking is valued.

Over time, as your lieutenants grow in confidence and competence, the business becomes less brittle, less prone to stall when you're unavailable.

---

2. Building a Brand Guidebook: Your Prince's Manual

In *The Prince*, Machiavelli provided an unflinching playbook for rulers. Your organization needs a comparable compendium—a living document that encapsulates your brand's strategy, standards, and operating principles. Think of this as the "Prince's Manual," so that any successor can understand, implement, and evolve your vision.

Core Sections of the Guidebook

1. **Vision, Mission, and Values**

   - **Vision Statement**: The aspirational north star—e.g., "To become the world's most trusted provider of premium home-health devices."

   - **Mission Pillars**: The three or four fundamental promises you deliver (quality, innovation, customer first, sustainability).

   - **Cultural Values**: The behaviors and mindsets you prize—agility, integrity, mastery of detail, data-driven rigor.

2. **Brand Identity and Voice**

   - **Visual Guidelines**: Logos, color palettes, typography, image style. Include templates for packaging, listing images, social media posts, and storefront banners.

   - **Copy Frameworks**: Tone of voice rules—direct, authoritative, empathetic—and archetypal messaging structures for titles, bullets, A+ Content, email outreach.

3. **Product Development Playbook**

   - **Research Criteria**: Market signals, margin thresholds, competitive gap analysis steps.

   - **Supplier Selection Process**: Evaluation rubrics, quality audit checklists, contract templates.

   - **Iteration Cycle**: How to collect feedback, prioritize improvements, and roll out updated versions.

4. **Go-to-Market and Growth Strategies**

   - **Launch Blueprint**: Pre-launch checklist, timing windows, ad strategy, review seeding plan.

   - **Scaling Tactics**: When and how to expand ad budgets, introduce variations, leverage external traffic, and optimize international rollouts.

5. **Customer Experience Standards**

   - **Service Protocols**: Response time SLAs, tone guidelines, escalation paths for complex issues.

   - **Crisis Playbooks**: Rapid-response scripts for product defects, listing suppressions, trademark claims.

6. **Performance Management and Reporting**

   - **KPI Definitions and Targets**: Clear formulas for ACOS, TACoS, conversion rate, return rate, and who tracks them.

   - **Reporting Cadence**: Daily dashboards, weekly business reviews, monthly strategy check-ins.

7. **Governance and Compliance**

   - **Amazon Policy Tracker**: How to stay updated on TOS changes and implement necessary SOP tweaks.

   - **Legal and IP Assets**: Trademark, patent, and distributor agreement registries, including renewal calendars.

8. **Succession Planning**

- **Role Descriptions and Career Paths**: Profiles for each leadership role, required competencies, development goals.

- **Onboarding Roadmap**: Step-by-step plan for bringing in new managers, culminating in certification based on practical assessments.

This manual becomes the single source of truth for how your brand operates. Share it widely, encourage feedback, and treat it as a living document—updating it whenever you refine a process or shift strategy.

---

3. From Operator to Owner: Installing Managers, SOPs, Incentive Structures

Machiavelli reminded princes that institutions, not individuals, sustain power. To shift from hands-on operator to strategic owner, you must delegate operational duties completely, install strong leadership, codify processes into SOPs, and align everyone's incentives with your long-term objectives.

Hiring and Empowering Managers

- **Define Leadership Roles**
  Identify the key management positions needed: Head of Operations, Head of Marketing, Head of Customer Experience, Head of Finance. Craft precise job

descriptions that blend functional expertise with cultural fit.

- **Select for Judgment and Alignment**
  In addition to technical skills, assess candidates for their ability to make sound decisions under ambiguity and their resonance with your brand's values. Use case-study interviews—present real past challenges and ask how they would respond.

- **Grant Authority with Accountability**
  For each manager, delineate their decision budget—the financial thresholds and scope within which they can act without further approval. Tie these to clear performance metrics and review them regularly.

- **Champion Coaching over Command**
  As the owner, shift from giving direct orders to serving as mentor and strategic advisor. Hold monthly one-on-one strategy sessions, review their teams' performance, and unblock obstacles, rather than micromanaging day-to-day.

Embedding SOPs Across the Organization

- **Centralize SOP Documentation**
  Keep all SOPs in an accessible, version-controlled system (e.g., a shared wiki or knowledge base). Use approval workflows so updates are reviewed by relevant stakeholders before going live.

- **Train and Certify**
  New hires must complete SOP-based training modules

and pass practical exams before handling live tasks. Offer refreshers quarterly to ensure everyone stays current as processes evolve.

- **Audit Compliance**
  Assign a rotating "Process Owner" for each SOP, responsible for quarterly audits. They check that steps are followed, data is recorded correctly, and outcomes meet targets. Any deviations trigger root-cause analyses and SOP revisions.

Crafting Incentive Structures

Machiavelli wrote that a prince's subjects must sense that their interests align with his own. Your team's rewards should therefore mirror the health and growth of the business.

- **Balanced Scorecards for Managers**
  Combine metrics for short-term performance (e.g., monthly sales targets, ACOS limits, customer satisfaction scores) with long-term goals (e.g., new product success rates, process improvement milestones, team development).

- **Profit-Sharing or Equity Stakes**
  Offer high-performing managers a share of annual profits or a path to small equity grants. This turns them from hired hands into invested partners who benefit directly when the business thrives—and suffer alongside you if it falters.

- **Team-Level Rewards**
  When a launch hits targets, or customer feedback reaches new highs, celebrate with team bonuses, off-site retreats, or public recognition. These rituals build camaraderie and reinforce collective ownership.

---

4. Ensuring Continuity and Evolution

Even the best succession plans fail if the new leadership resists change or operates in isolation. To ensure continuity and ongoing improvement:

- **Transition Timeline**
  Create a multi-phase plan:

    1. **Co-Leadership Phase**: You and your successor jointly steer the business for 3–6 months.

    2. **Advisory Phase**: You step back to a quarterly advisor role, intervening only for strategic or crisis decisions.

    3. **Honorary Phase**: You remain as a non-executive chairperson, attending annual reviews and serving as brand ambassador.

- **Knowledge Transfer Rituals**
  Host monthly "Leadership Councils" where managers present deep dives on their domains, discuss upcoming

challenges, and surface ideas. Record these sessions to build an institutional memory.

- **Continuous Innovation Forums**
  Encourage teams to submit "Invention Proposals"—new product ideas, marketing experiments, process automations. Hold quarterly pitch days where the best concepts receive dedicated funding.

By architecting both the handover and the mechanisms for ongoing adaptation, you guarantee that your Amazon empire doesn't merely survive your exit—it flourishes under the stewardship of the next generation.

Conclusion: Your Legacy, Secured

Machiavelli's ultimate test for a prince was the durability of his rule after his departure. For the Amazon entrepreneur, true success lies not only in dominating the marketplace today but in building an organization that can outlast any single individual. By meticulously training your team, codifying your strategy into a comprehensive guidebook, empowering skilled managers with robust SOPs and aligned incentives, and structuring a phased transition, you transform from an indispensable operator into a visionary owner whose legacy continues through capable successors. In doing so, you honor Machiavelli's enduring insight: power consolidated in institutions, not personalities, is the only power that endures.

Conclusion: Machiavelli for the Modern Seller

The world of Amazon selling is a crucible of fierce competition, swift upheaval, and relentless demand for results. Here, the lessons of Machiavelli's *The Prince* ring truer than ever. Over the course of this book, we've seen how the modern seller must combine ruthless action with deft perception; how they must wield control like a weapon yet bend with the winds of change; and how, above all, they must embrace the hard truths that Machiavelli laid bare:

> "It is much safer to be feared than loved, if one must choose."

> "Everyone sees what you appear to be, few experience what you really are."

> "Fortune favors the bold, not the faint of heart."

These aphorisms speak directly to the heart of ecommerce: Amazon rewards courage, punishes hesitation, and offers no mercy to the naive.

Ruthlessness Balanced by Perception

At the core of Machiavellian strategy lies the paradox of **ruthlessness tempered by appearance**. On one hand, you must outmaneuver competitors with decisive price moves, aggressive launches, and unrelenting defense of your listings. You must slash underperforming SKUs without regret, wield automated repricers like battering rams, and use legal and policy tools to eliminate hijackers and counterfeiters. This is the ruthless half of the equation: the unglamorous, behind-the-scenes actions that secure and expand your power.

Yet ruthlessness alone will not sustain you. Machiavelli cautioned that a prince must **appear** virtuous, even when his deeds are merciless:

> "Everyone sees what you appear to be, few
> experience what you really are."

In practice, this means your storefront, your images, your A+ Content, and your customer communications must radiate integrity, expertise, and care. Your unboxing experience, your packaging inserts, your prompt customer responses—these are your public face. They project warmth, reliability, and quality. They win the trust of buyers who know nothing of your hard bargaining with suppliers or your cutthroat pricing strategies. By balancing raw ambition with polished optics, you create a fortress no competitor can storm: a brand that feels bulletproof.

Control Tempered by Agility

Machiavelli lauded the prince who governs with order and institutions:

> "The main foundations of all states are good laws and
> good arms."

For the Amazon seller, institutions take the form of SOPs,
automated systems, and a trained team that can execute
flawlessly. These are your "good laws," the documented
procedures that ensure every launch, every ad campaign, and
every inventory reorder follows best practices. Your "good arms"
are the tools—repricers, analytics platforms, outsourced
agencies—that extend your reach and safeguard your operations.

But no fortress stands if its gates are unmanned or its walls sealed
against the changing seasons. Therefore, control must be **agile**.
You must move faster than your competitors to exploit trending
keywords, adjust to an unannounced Amazon policy change, or
pivot your ad spend when costs suddenly spike. As Machiavelli
reminds us:

> "Fortune is a woman, and if you wish to keep her
> under it is necessary to beat and ill-use her; and it is
> seen that she allows herself to be mastered by the
> violent rather than by the timid."

In other words, you cannot simply set up your systems and hope
for consistent returns. You must monitor performance metrics in
real time, run quick experiments, and pull the trigger on decisions
with a bias for action. Your institutions give you stability; your
agility ensures those institutions remain relevant in an
environment that never stops shifting.

Amazon Rewards the Bold, Punishes the Naive

Every chapter of this book has underscored one indisputable fact: Amazon is not a charity. It does not reward sincerity, longevity, or sheer good intent. It rewards those who seize opportunities and punish those who hesitate. It elevates the listing that generates rapid sales velocity, the brand that commands glowing reviews with surgical precision, and the seller who maintains perfect Buy Box share through a combination of price strategy and logistical excellence.

Machiavelli observed:

> "He who is highly esteemed is not easily conspired against."

On Amazon, esteem is earned by metrics. A listing with thousands of positive, recent reviews and a consistently high conversion rate becomes difficult for new entrants to dislodge. Yet that esteem evaporates overnight the moment you let your guard down—when your stockouts spike, your ad spend wanes, or your response times slip.

Meanwhile, sellers who invade with audacity—who launch into under-optimized niches with bold branding, who exploit seasonal windows with lightning deals, who disrupt categories with new bundles—often find themselves rewarded with outsized algorithmic favor. They become the unexpected princes of their segments, leveraging momentum to build near-untouchable positions.

Be the Prince Your Business Needs—or Watch Someone Else Take Your Throne

The final call, then, is this: **Embody the Machiavellian spirit in every aspect of your Amazon venture**. Lead with decisive action. Fortify your brand's perception. Build institutions that scale. Stay agile in the face of Amazon's caprices. And when the moment demands it, act ruthlessly—pruning failing SKUs, outpricing competitors, and deploying every tool at your disposal.

Do not delude yourself into believing that good intentions will carry you. Do not wait for perfect conditions. Do not build your house on rented land without a plan for expansion beyond the marketplace. Machiavelli's counsel is stark:

> "It is better to act and repent than not to act and regret."

So act. Seize your niche. Command your category. Write your own rules, then adapt them as the terrain shifts. Because on Amazon, you either **take the throne**—become the undisputed seller in your domain—or you **watch someone else** ascend in your place.

Be the prince your business needs. Rule with vision, strength, and the cunning to survive whatever Fortune throws your way. Or be prepared to bow before a new ruler who will.

THIS IS NOT A COLLECTION

This volume is part of **Ancient Wisdom Hacks**—
an ongoing body of work focused on how strategy, power, and
failure actually function under pressure.

The books are only one layer.

What you are reading is an entry point into a larger system of
interpretation, application, and expansion.

WHAT THESE WORKS ARE DESIGNED TO DO

Most people look for answers.

These works expose patterns:

- How decisions are made before they are visible
- How systems weaken before they collapse
- How power shifts before it is recognized

This is not theory.
It is applied observation.

THE SYSTEM BEHIND THE WORK

Across all volumes and future releases, three forces remain
constant:

- **Strategy** — how outcomes are shaped before action
- **Conflict** — how people and systems break under pressure
- **Power** — how control is gained, maintained, and lost

No single book contains the full picture.
Each adds another angle.

CONTINUE BEYOND THIS VOLUME

New interpretations, applied volumes, and extended works are released continuously.

To access current and future material, visit:

www.AncientWisdomHacks.com

WHAT YOU WILL FIND

- Additional applied volumes across industries
- Expanded interpretations of foundational texts
- New releases not available through standard distribution
- Future projects extending beyond books

The system is still expanding.

FINAL POSITION

Clarity does not make outcomes easier.

It removes the illusion that they were ever simple.

Ancient Wisdom Hacks
Interpretation over repetition.
Application over theory.